W9-ABH-438

SKILFUL MEANS

SKILFUL MEANS

A Concept in Mahayana Buddhism

MICHAEL PYE

ST. JOSEPH'S UNIVERSITY

3 9353 00243 1508

DUCKWORTH

BQ
4370
P93

First published in 1978 by Gerald Duckworth & Co. Ltd.
The Old Piano Factory, 43 Gloucester Crescent, London NW1

Distributed in the USA by Southwest Book Services, Inc
5941 Top Line Drive, Dallas, Texas, 75247

© 1978 by Michael Pye

All rights reserved. No part of this publication may be reproduced, stored in a
retrieval system, or transmitted, in any form or by any means electronic,
mechanical, photocopying, recording or otherwise, without the prior
permission of the publisher.

ISBN 0 7156   1266 2

Printed in England by
Stephen Austin & Sons Ltd., Hertford.

CONTENTS

ACKNOWLEDGEMENTS

So many persons are karmically involved, so to speak, in the coming about of this book, that it is quite impossible to list them. Indeed there are thousands whose names I do not know. As examples, however, I should like to thank my teacher at Cambridge, Maurice Wiles, who suggested I went to Japan to see what I would find, Raymond Hammer who helped me to put the suggestion into effect, and Carmen Blacker who conveyed in advance that Japanese Buddhism is both subtle and entertaining. I was singularly fortunate in being lodged at first with Iyanaga Shōkichi and his family in Tokyo; and their relaxed guidance was complemented by the aid of many other Japanese friends and informants, as I eventually developed an interest in the Buddhist concept of skilful means. The matter has concerned me now for many years among other duties, but an appointment to the Department of Religious Studies at the University of Lancaster, headed then at its inception by Ninian Smart, gave me the chance to pursue it more systematically. A second journey to Japan, relative to this and other projects, was partly financed by the University of Lancaster and the Spalding Trust, to whom my thanks are accorded. The subsequent patience of John Tinsley and other colleagues at the University of Leeds allowed me to complete my work, and particular thanks are due to Elizabeth Hart, Dorothy Raper and Hazel Walker for much cheerful perseverance at the typewriter. I am grateful also to Carmen Blacker, Inagaki Hisao and Ninian Smart for comments leading to some corrections.

Two formal but no less grateful acknowledgements should be made; firstly to the Kōsei Press in Tokyo who kindly allowed me to base my quotations from The Lotus Sutra on their recently published translation (details below); and secondly to Edward Conze, both for his own incidental encouragement and especially for the loan of a privately circulated draft translation of The Teaching of Vimalakīrti, made by the late R. H. Robinson, which was particularly helpful in the formulation of quotations from that writing. To avoid misunderstanding, the above sources have not usually been quoted as such but freely and critically drawn upon, so that while the debt is great the responsibility lies here.

This writing has been a personal interest for so many years that readers may forgive me for adding thanks to my wife Christine for her many favours.

M.P.

CONVENTIONS

(i)   Since Sanskrit is the lingua franca for Mahayana Buddhism, Sanskrit terms are freely used without necessarily implying a Sanskrit source. Some very common terms such as bodhisattva, nirvana, dharma, karma, buddha, and sutra are accepted as anglicised, and diacritical marks are omitted.

(ii)   Pali forms are sometimes used when the context demands it, and again some very common ones are anglicised, e.g. dhamma, sutta.

(iii)   When used with a capital D, Dharma (or Pali, Dhamma) refers to the teaching proclaimed by the Buddha. When used with a small d, dharma, or dharmas, (Pali, dhamma(s)), refer to factors of existence as defined in Buddhist analysis.

(iv)   Proper nouns have usually been given diacritical marks as required, e.g. Vimalakīrti, except for the commonly anglicised Mahayana, Theravada, Pali, and Hinayana.

(v)   Except in special cases romanised Chinese follows the Wade-Giles system. Romanised Japanese follows the Hepburn system.

(vi)   Since some terms from all of the above four languages are indispensable, because of changing contexts, equivalents have sometimes been given in brackets with the abbreviations; Skt. (Sanskrit), P. (Pali), Ch. (Chinese) and J. (Japanese). It is hoped that enough have been given to signpost the reader without ruining the text by putting them in all the time.

(vii)   Names of sutras frequently used are given in an easy conventionalised English form, such as The Lotus Sutra. The relationship between various names for the main sources will be clear from Appendix A. Names of writings referred to incidentally are italicised.

(viii)   Chapters of sutras referred to with Arabic numerals are chapters in Sanskrit texts or translations thereof. Chapters of sutras referred to with Roman numerals are chapters in Chinese versions or translations thereof. Chapters referred to in words, e.g. 'Chapter Eight', refer to chapters in the present work.

(ix)   Japanese names are given surname first, except in a few cases where it is a writer who writes in a non-Japanese language and uses initials.

(x)   Chinese and Japanese characters have been restricted to the appendices and notes.

1 GENERAL INTRODUCTION

Buddhist skilful means

The concept of 'skilful means' is one of the leading ideas of Mahayana Buddhism and was first used extensively in The Lotus Sutra and other writings treated below. In Mahayana Buddhism the various forms of Buddhist teaching and practice are declared to be provisional means, all skilfully set up by the Buddha for the benefit of the unenlightened. A Buddhist who makes progress himself comes to recognise this provisional quality in the forms of his religion, and though using the means provided for him he has to learn not to be wrongly attached to them. He leaves them behind, like a raft left lying on the bank by a man who has crossed a stream and needs it no more. An advanced follower of Buddhism, usually named by Mahayana Buddhists a *bodhisattva*, continues to use such provisional means in order to lead other living things towards nirvana. A bodhisattva is skilled in allowing the Buddhist religion to be spelled out in all its detail, while not being ensnared by the false discriminations of the unenlightened.

'Skilful means' is a conflated term which is based on Chinese and Japanese usage, as explained later, and which refers to the overall spectrum of meanings with which we are concerned. Since 'skilful means' is about the way in which the goal, the intention, or the meaning of Buddhism is correlated with the unenlightened condition of living beings, it brings out particularly clearly how Mahayanists thought Buddhism, as a system, is supposed to be understood. Once established, the term continued to be used down to the present day, admittedly with some vagaries. It is fair to say that the method of thought and practice summed up by the concept of skilful means is one of the fundamental principles of Buddhism as a working religion. Indeed a Japanese writer has claimed that it is hardly possible to discuss Mahayana Buddhism at all without reference to it.[1]

Strangely enough the matter has never been the subject of extended study in the west. 'Nirvana', 'bodhisattva', 'emptiness' (Skt. *śūnyatā*) and so on have all been considered in this way and that, but apart from occasional references and brief definitions 'skilful means' has scarcely been attended to at all. A concept which has been used to explain the very existence of Buddhism as a functioning religious system demands closer attention. Even in the east there do not seem to have been any extended studies, and this may be partly due to the fact that Mahayanists have rather tended to take 'skilful means' for granted as a natural principle with which to regulate their

---

[1] Sawada Kenshō: 'Bukkyō ni okeru hōben no shisō ni tsuite' in *Bukkyō Bunka Kenkyū* 12 (1963) (沢田謙照, 仏教における[方便]の思想について, 仏教文化研究), p. 97. All Japanese names are given surname first.

religion. In recent times there have been a few shorter articles in Japanese, which have been quite useful to the present writer.[2] However even the Japanese have rather tended to deal with it *en passant* in their voluminous commentaries, and this has prevented the concept from emerging as one of central importance to Buddhist thought, in its own right.

When some years ago the writer visited the splendid headquarters of one of the lively new religions of modern Japan he was duly impressed with the architecture, the furnishings and the technology, the constant flow of people for counselling and devotions, the accessory organisations and the managerial

___

[2] Especially Sawada (see previous note); Masuda Hideo: 'Hannyakyō ni okeru "hōben" no imi ni tsuite' in *Indogaku Bukkyōgaku Kenkyū* No. 23 (1964) (増田英男, 般若経における [方便]の意昧について, 印度學佛教學研究), pp. 112-17; Kumoi Shōzen: 'Hōben to Shinjitsu' in Ōchō Keinichi (ed.), *Hokke Shisō*, Kyōto, 1969 (雲井昭善, 方便と真実 in 横超慧日, 法華思想). The following articles in denominational journals were not available: 大西泰信：[方便]の「波羅蜜」加行に関する一考察 駒沢宗学研究 1 (1956), pp. 152-4; 越智淳仁：究竟は方便なり in 密教学会報 6 (1967), pp. 25-29; 種田哲也：往生論註における 般若と方便—特に阿弥陀仏論の論理的根拠に in 真宗学 27/28 (1962), pp. 167-178; 普賢大円：親鸞教学に於ける方便の意義 in 真宗研究 7 (1956), pp. 21-31. In 1974 an article in English by Daigan and Alicia Matsunaga appeared in the *Japanese Journal of Religious Studies*, Vol. I No. 1, pp. 51-72, entitled 'The Concept of Upāya 方便 in Mahayana Buddhist Philosophy'. It picks out the general characteristics of the concept quite interestingly, though it must be said that the historical bearings are rather vague. In particular the thrusting back of the Mahayana concept of skilful means (Skt. *upāya*) into the initial development of Buddhism is carried through in a rather unhistorical way, as indeed it was in Alicia Matsunaga's fascinating earlier volume *The Buddhist Philosophy of Assimilation, The Historical Development of the Honji Suijaku Theory*, Tokyo 1969 (cf. my review article 'Assimilation and skilful means' touching on this very point in *Religion, Journal of Religion and Religions*, 1, 2 (1971). The difficulty is that the term *upāya* is hardly used at all in the Pali texts, whereas it emerged as a technical term in the early Mahayana re-statements. Of course the Mahayana viewpoint is that this is how early Buddhism is to be understood, and there is much to be said for the viewpoint (cf. Chapter Seven below); but while it is right to stress the importance of the Buddha's very decision to teach at all, it is misleading to suggest that the Buddha in person understood his work specifically in terms of *upāya* (article named above, p. 53) as there is no historical evidence for this whatever. The argument should be that the technical term 'skilful means' is one which the Mahayanists reasonably applied in retrospect to the fundamental character of Buddhism as it was first conceived. Another most important historical point is that the term *upāya* is very little used in texts ascribed to Nāgārjuna (the Matsunagas give not one explicit quotation), though it is quite common in the basic Mahayana sutras which *pre-date* his work. We can positively state that the equivalent *fang-pien* appears once only in the *Chung-lun* (T1546) and then not in the verses ascribed to Nāgārjuna but in the commentary (see Chapter Six below). Of course the concept of *upāya* is not unrelated to Nāgārjuna's account of two kinds of truth, but the latter is historically secondary. It would in no way detract from the strength of the interpretative position (which is what the Matsunagas' article really reflects) if the historical phases were more clearly and accurately delineated. Although the study presented here was first undertaken some time ago and is conceived along rather different lines, Alicia Matsunaga's *The Buddhist Philosophy of Assimilation* certainly underlines the importance of this whole subject for understanding Buddhism, and it contains much interesting material of which some is referred to again with gratitude below. Other works in European languages deal with the term skilful means (Skt. *upāya*, etc.) even more incidentally, although the first brief discussion was in the appendix volume of M. E. Burnouf's pioneer translation of The Lotus Sutra, *Le Lotus de la Bonne Loi, Vol. II Appendice* (*Mémoires Annexes*), Paris 1852 (2nd ed.. 1925), pp. 549 ff.

efficiency, the obvious emphasis on cheerful prosperity and on daily personal well-being. It was radically unlike the dimly lit temples in the old style, their cemeteries crowded and overgrown, their mournful bells echoing the half-understood and half-forgotten secrets of traditional Buddhism. These notes of transience and quiescence were far from the minds of the coachloads of well-dressed and optimistically chattering housewives attending their modern mecca in central Tokyo. Their concern was rather with family affairs, schooling, cultural and leisure pursuits, and the elimination of factors inconsistent with well-being. Nevertheless beneath all the usual appurtenances of a modern religion this particular movement was concerned, my guide explained, to teach 'true Buddhism'. In reality there was here, he went on, no so-called 'new' religion at all, but an ancient one. Then how was the coexistence of these seemingly diverse directions to be understood? That, it was explained, is a matter of skilful means.[3]

This account was no modern simplification or sectarian perversion. The Lotus Sutra, a Mahayana Buddhist text dating from about two thousand years ago, explained that the Buddha himself uses 'innumerable devices' to lead living beings along and to separate them from their attachments.[4] Such devices are formulated in terms of the relative ignorance and the passionate attachments of those who need them, but they turn and dissolve into the Buddhist attainment of release. Similarly the great celestial bodhisattvas or buddhas-to-be are characterised not only by their penetrating insight into

---

[3] It should be noted that the explanation was not an official one, and the term was introduced when the discussion became one step removed from a direct account of practice and doctrine. The movement in question was the Risshō Kōsei kai (立正佼成会), a modern ecumenically-minded lay movement based mainly on the Tendai-Nichirenite tradition. The term 'skilful means' (J. *hōben* 方便) was clearly present in the mind of the person concerned as a result of regular reading of The Lotus Sutra, which is to be considered in detail below.

[4] T IX 5c (無數方便) cf. KSS 32. All references to The Lotus Sutra will give the location for Kumārajīva's Chinese version in the *Taishō Shinshū Daizōkyō* 大正新脩大藏經 (*The Tripitaka in Chinese*), ed. J. Takakusu and K. Watanabe, 1927, 1960² Tokyo, (abbreviated to T, followed by volume, page and horizontal column). A reference is also given to the recently published English translation by Kato, Soothill and Schiffer, abbreviated to KSS, which is the first integral translation of Kumārajīva's Chinese text into a European language, entitled *Myōhō-Renge-Kyō The Sutra of the Lotus Flower of the Wonderful Law*, Tokyo 1971. Although some criticisms could no doubt be made, and the translation has not always been closely followed in quotations given below, it is quite adequate for the general orientation of English readers. Its use in quotations below is by kind permission of the Kōsei Publishing Company, Tokyo. (This translation has since appeared in a new edition from John Weatherhill, Inc. Tokyo.) The present discussion does not assume responsibility for a general introduction to The Lotus Sutra or its contents, and is directed only towards the concept of 'skilful means'. Readers who wish to examine the wider context of this argument in the literature itself would be advised to begin with a reading of the above-mentioned translation, which is preferable to H. Kern's translation from a Buddhist Hybrid Sanskrit text (the language in which it was originally composed), *Saddharma-Puṇḍarīka or The Lotus of the True Law*, Oxford 1884 (Max Müller ed. *Sacred Books of the East* Vol. XXI), reprinted New York 1963. Kern's translation is now out of date and unsatisfactory for various reasons, although alas it has still not been superseded as a translation from Sanskrit. The KSS translation is admittedly from a Chinese version, but one which became important as a text in its own right.

the true nature of reality but also by a great compassion for suffering beings. They too deploy a range of methods for the salvation of the multitude, skilfully tuning them to a variety of needs yet consistently intimating the intention of nirvana. The release of all sentient beings is guaranteed in the nirvana of any one bodhisattva, a nirvana postponed and yet assured. For one thing the great vow of a bodhisattva bears all suffering beings along with him. For another thing, to imagine that one being or some beings could attain nirvana, and not others, would fall some way short of the radical teaching that all phenomena are equally void of persistent ontological status, or that, as The Lotus Sutra puts it, all things are nirvanic from the beginning.[5] The path of a bodhisattva is to know this, and at the same time to keep on playing the game of skilful means to save people from themselves. This style of thinking, in which insight (Skt. *prajñā*)[6] and means (Skt. *upāya*) are inextricably related, is the key to understanding the proliferation of new forms which the Mahayana has woven across half Asia.

It is also possible to look at skilful means not from the side of the Buddhas and bodhisattvas who invent them, but from the side of the sentient beings who need them, that is, from the point of view of human beings ignorantly entangled in the apparently ceaseless round of birth and death (Skt. *saṃsāra*). Indeed Sawada Kenshō reflected a common Japanese assumption about the matter when he concluded in a short article that there are two basic meanings to be remembered. The first is skilful means as invented by the Buddha for the benefit of sentient beings. The second is skilful means as used by sentient beings for the attainment of nirvana or release (J. *gedatsu*).[7] The means themselves are the same, of course, whichever idea is uppermost.

Whether considered as working downwards or upwards the skilful means are above all provisional. They not only need to be established from above but also to be superseded from below. As the beneficiaries become enlightened the expedients become redundant. This process may be a rather rough dismantling and debunking as in some corridors of the Zen tradition, or it may be a smooth transference from one level of meaning to another. Since the skilful means are initially tuned in to the needs of beings entangled in ignorance and *saṃsāra*, it is quite natural that release from these involves a subtle change in the significance or status of the very means which bring it about. In this sense the concept of skilful means involves the paradox that Mahayana Buddhism elaborates and proliferates itself without end as a

---

[5] T IX 8b, (諸法從本來常自寂滅相). 'All dharmas are themselves permanently nirvanic from the beginning', cf. KSS 54 'All existence, from the beginning, Is ever of the nirvana-nature.' The characters 寂滅 (J. *jaku-metsu*) used here are frequently used to translate the Sanskrit term nirvana, which is also often merely transliterated as 涅槃 (J. *nehan*) e.g. in the immediate context quoted here.

[6] *Prajñā* is commonly translated 'wisdom', but 'insight' is marginally preferable as being less misleading. The former tends to suggest in English a body of accumulated knowledge, sometimes moralising, while 'insight' adequately conveys the idea of penetratingly seeing the true nature of things. Cf. below, Chapter Six, note 1.

[7] Sawada Kenshō, *op. cit. Gedatsu:* 解脱.

religion of salvation and at the same time it tends towards its own dissolution.

Indeed the Mahayanists claim, and not without some justice, that 'skilful means' is the key to the understanding of Buddhism in general. Perhaps the most suggestive passages in this connection are those which narrate the Buddha's initial decision to teach at all (cf. Chapter Seven below). Without this decision the Buddhist religion would never have developed any articulate form whatever. It is therefore of great importance that Mahayanists interpret it in terms of the Buddha's skilful means. For them this key concept is the appropriate way in which to understand any phase of Buddhism which is supposed to derive from the Buddha's initiative, whether it be abstractedly conceptual, concretely narrative, or expressed as meditational practice. The 'answers' which Buddhism apparently offers, such as the teaching of cessation (Skt. *nirodha*) or nirvana, are devised entirely in terms of the problem and they are not intended to have any particular meaning beyond the attainment of the solution. Thus 'Buddhism', as a specific religion identifiable in human history, is a skilful means.

The pages which follow are a systematic attempt to get clear what a skilful means is.

The literature of skilful means

The modern printed edition of the canonical writings of Chinese and Japanese Buddhism runs into a total of eighty five thick volumes. Many of these contain different versions of Indian writings which were translated several times by different people. Since all of these are preserved in the 'Great Store of Sutras' (J. *Daizōkyō*)[8] innumerable miles of print lie more or less unused in East Asia itself and it is quite appropriate and indeed necessary for the student to be selective. Two criteria are adopted here, namely coherence of language, which means in practice restriction to works produced by one translator, and frequency of use of the writings. In this way a coherent and more or less manageable set of texts was defined, which may be taken as fairly representing the thought of Mahayana Buddhism in East Asia.

As to the translator, the obvious choice is Kumārajīva, whose work dominates the transmission of Mahayana Buddhism from India to China. Much of his life was spent in Central Asia. He was born in 344 at Kucha, which lies about half way between Kashmir and the western end of the Great Wall of China, on the northern route through the Tarim Basin. His mother was a local 'princess' and his father was Indian. It appears that he was turned over to monastic life at the age of six or seven, and that he was instructed in Hinayana Buddhism in Kashmir and in Mahayana Buddhism at Kashgar. For about thirty years he lived at Kucha, but in 383 or 385 he was taken off to China by a Chinese military force, arriving eventually at Ch'ang An. He lived here probably from 401 until his death in 413, apparently in some

---

[8] For our purposes this is the *Taishō Shinshū Daizōkyō*, cf. note 4, though of course earlier printed editions also exist.

style, working with others on translations of Mahayana texts from Sanskrit
into Chinese.[9] Quite apart from his translating activity Kumārajīva played
a leading role in discussions about the right understanding of Mahayana
Buddhism, which had first arisen in the context of Indian Buddhism in
general ('Hinayana') but which was now being stated in a language hitherto
used for Taoist concepts. Since he has always been respected as a fair
exponent of Mahayana his translations are a particularly useful basis of
discussion.

There are some famous texts which Kumārajīva did not translate, for
example, The Laṅkāvatāra Sutra, which is the first statement in anonymous
sutra form of the mind-only or consciousness-only style within Mahayana
Buddhism (defined eventually as the Yogācāra School, but having a wide
influence on Tantric Buddhism and on Ch'an or Zen).[10] There are other
sutras which he translated but of which a different translation is in common
use in Japan today, for example, The Heart Sutra.[11] Nevertheless it is his
versions which are generally used for three of the most widespread Mahayana
sutras of all, namely The Lotus Sutra, The Teaching of Vimalakīrti, and The
Diamond Sutra. He translated two longer forms of The Perfection of Insight
Sutra, namely that in '8000' lines and that in '25000' lines. He spent much
effort, presumably, over the massive commentary on the latter, The Great
Treatise on the Perfection of Insight, ascribed perhaps with greater piety
than accuracy to the Mahayana thinker Nāgārjuna. With this belong three
other works which also align Kumārajīva with Nāgārjuna's Mādhyamika
school, which was followed more specifically in China and Japan by the
'Three Treatise School'.[12] The three are The Middle Treatise, The Twelve
Topic Treatise and The Hundred Treatise. In all his work covers both
popular and intellectual aspects of Mahayana Buddhism. A brief introductory
note on each of the works used here is given in Appendix A.

The Teaching of Vimalakīrti is simply not extant in Sanskrit, but on what
grounds does an investigation of The Lotus Sutra follow Kumārajīva's
version? There are two main reasons. The first is that it effectively became a
religious text in its own right as far as the world of Sino-Japanese Buddhism
was concerned and is to this day far more widely used than any Sanskrit

---

[9] Demiéville, P. et al. (eds.) *Hōbōgirin, Dictionnaire Encyclopédique du Bouddhisme
d'après les Sources Chinoises et Japonaises*, Paris and Tokyo 1929 ff., *Fascicule Annexe* p. 144.
Some alternative dates are also given. Kumārajīva is the Indian form of his name, which is
rendered in Chinese characters as 鳩摩羅什 and sometimes abbreviated to 羅什 (J. Kumarajū
and Rajū, respectively). Cf. also Robinson, R. H. *Early Mādhyamika in India and China*,
Madison, Milwaukee and London 1967, pp. 72-73, for more details and variant dates.

[10] Known to English readers through Suzuki Daisetsu's translation *The Lankavatara Sutra*,
London 1932 and also his *Studies in the Lankavatara Sutra*, London 1930.

[11] The one mostly used is the version by Hsüan Tsang (T251); Kumārajīva's version is
T250. These numbers identify works by the order in which they appear in the *Daizōkyō*, but
the correlation of works with bound volumes is effected by means of a catalogue: *Hōbōgirin's
Fascicule Annexe* (note 9 above), or the *Taishō Shinshū Daizōkyō Mokuroku* in one small
volume, Tokyo 1969.

[12] 三論宗 Ch. *San-lun-tsung*, J. *San-ron-shū*.

original. The second reason is that the 'original' Buddhist Hybrid Sanskrit text is very unstable. For one thing there is still no agreed critical edition which adequately collates the various manuscripts and fragments, and in addition it has become clear that the sutra as a whole is the result of a piecemeal process of compilation which is still imperfectly understood (for a summary account see Appendix B). Even if one could be reasonably certain of distinct stages in the growth of the sutra in terms of verse passages, prose passages, and earlier and later chapters, it scarcely seems possible as yet to proceed backwards to an 'original' Lotus Sutra. Nor is there any particular stage in its presumed compilation at which one would have any strong reason to freeze the historical analysis in the interests of finally studying the ideas. If the text were taken at its largest extent it would be very difficult to define historically the persons for whom it was meaningful in that form, e.g. third century inhabitants of Kucha or eleventh century Nepalese. One would in any case have to locate it *after* the initial growth of Mahayana Buddhism, which is reflected in, and indeed known to us because of the gradual compilation of texts just such as this. There are also knotty problems about the interrelated growth of The Lotus Sutra, The Perfection of Insight Sutras and others, which are still most imperfectly understood. There is a continuous danger of circular arguments about the priority of this or that part of various texts and the way in which the same texts are carved up to reconstruct a compilation process. Because of this morass of little studied and probably permanently intractable problems the present enquiry into *an idea* shifted, or rather reverted, to the much more clearly defined and above all unified texts of Sino-Japanese Buddhism. The contents of the texts which Kumārajīva translated had a definite and coherent meaning for him and his associates; and they provide, in the form in which they are available to us, a significant sample of the ideas current among all later East Asian Buddhists. If specialists in some one or other of the Buddhist Hybrid Sanskrit 'originals' have observations or qualifications about the pre-Chinese history of this idea, they will of course be of interest. It is anticipated however that such comments are most unlikely to affect the overall picture very much; and it may be assumed subject to correction that the main outlines of 'skilful means' thinking given below reflect not only Kumārajīva's mind (for he believed in what he translated) but also, since his reception of Indian Mahayana is generally taken to be intellectually accurate, present a fair impression of the meaning of the term in pre-Chinese Mahayana.

To some extent Kumārajīva put his own stamp on the writings which he translated. He was not a fussy literalist. It will be explained below, for example, that he was careless of the distinction between *upāya* ('means') and *upāya-kauśalya* ('skill-in-means'). R. H. Robinson made a detailed study of Kumārajīva's translation methods and concluded that the number and the type of mistakes in his work were not such as to lead to any significant misunderstanding of the original.[13] Robinson also studied what can be

[13] Robinson, *op. cit.* pp. 77-88.

determined of Kumārajīva's own thought, on the basis of his words recorded
by others and some correspondence with Hui-yuan, and concluded that
Kumārajīva was broadly sympathetic to the Mahayana in general while
placing a particular reliance on the Mādhyamika school of interpretation.[14]
Since Kumārajīva had a clear grasp of Mahayana principles, the texts
translated by him provide a coherent and reliable corpus for any avenues of
investigation which are representative of East Asian Mahayana Buddhism
in general.

　　The number of texts said to have been translated by Kumārajīva ranges
from just over thirty to over one hundred (including no doubt false ascrip-
tions to win prestige for some other translations),[15] but even on a low count
it would be difficult to study all in equal detail. The second criterion of
selection is therefore the frequency with which various writings were and are
used. This cannot be exactly calculated, of course, but there is no doubt that
the sutras already mentioned above were and are some of the most commonly
used in Mahayana Buddhism. The Lotus Sutra and The Teaching of Vimalakīrti were widely current in Central Asia and China and are still very well
known in contemporary Japan.[16] Their contents are familiar to both monks
and laymen. Particular devotion is paid to The Lotus Sutra in the Tendai
(Ch. T'ien T'ai) and Nichirenite sects of Japanese Buddhism. At the same
time The Lotus Sutra is one of the classical statements of Mahayana universalism and is recognised as such by Buddhists of diverse denominations.[17]
The Teaching of Vimalakīrti is not linked with any specific sect as such but
it has always been particularly popular among laymen, perhaps because its
leading figure, Vimalakīrti, is himself a layman. Because they are so well
known these two texts form the main material for what follows.

　　The Lotus Sutra is, in an important sense, mainly about 'skilful means',

---

[14] *Op. cit.* pp. 88-95.

[15] *Op. cit.* pp. 73-77. cf. *Hōbōgirin, Fascicule Annexe*, p. 144, where 57 works are listed.

[16] On archaeological evidence for the popularity of The Lotus Sutra in Central Asia and
North-Western China (including a close association with the Teaching of Vimalakīrti) see
Davidson, J. Leroy, *The Lotus Sutra in Chinese Art*, New Haven U.S.A. 1954, and on its
importance in early Japanese Buddhism see De Visser, *Ancient Buddhism in Japan*, Tokyo
1935; and of course there are many miscellaneous indications for both writings.

[17] The progressive specialisation of East Asian Buddhism into schools and sects did not
make the use of particular sutras as tightly compartmentalised as one might at first imagine.
The Lotus Sutra, for example, was by no means confined to the Tendai Sect and its deriv-
atives, but continued to be known to Pure Land Buddhists and Zen Buddhists, and to have
a broad cultural impact. The Heart Sutra is used more or less across the board. At the same
time the result of any extensive study of ancient sutras does not necessarily directly reflect
the mental activity of any one group of Buddhists empirically defined within society at one
point in history. Results should rather be taken into account as a factor in long-term cultural
impact. For example, although the three sutras specially used in Pure Land Buddhism are
not examined in detail here, and although Pure Land Buddhists do not in practice make *much*
use of other sutras, one could still argue that the central ideas of Mahayana Buddhism in
general, as expressed in the sutras which have been studied, are relevant to any really satis-
factory understanding of the Pure Land denominations.

and no apology is made for treating it in some detail in Chapters Two to Four below. The Teaching of Vimalakīrti is treated by itself in Chapter Five. It is shorter than The Lotus Sutra but provides an important link with The Perfection of Insight and dependent literature, which is taken up in Chapter Six. The Lotus Sutra is also taken up again in Chapter Seven where some passages are treated in the section on the Buddha's decision to teach *Dhamma* (Skt. *Dharma*). The purpose of this is to indicate the matrix of Mahayana principles in early Buddhism.

The Lotus Sutra and The Teaching of Vimalakīrti have a relatively large number of occurrences of the term 'skilful means', and these are to some extent concentrated in important chapters. In each case it is the second chapter which gives the tone for the writing as a whole, after a more or less mythological scenario has been painted in the introductory first chapter. In each case, too, the second chapter bears the explicit title 'Skilful Means'. As a brief generalisation one might say that in The Lotus Sutra the emphasis is on interpreting the way in which the Buddha himself is believed to have taught, while in The Teaching of Vimalakīrti it is on the style of life of a bodhisattva following the path of the Buddha. Between them the two sutras also reflect quite well both the intellectual and the popular aspects of Mahayana Buddhism. The bodhisattva Mañjuśrī, for example, is supposed to be the epitome of the virtue of insight (Skt. *prajñā*), and his discussion with Vimalakīrti is a classical and not yet scholastic statement of the teaching of voidness (Skt. *śūnyatā*). The bodhisattva Avalokiteśvara, by contrast, is particularly symbolic of the many forms taken by Buddhist compassion (Skt. *karuṇā*) in the popular mind, while the chapter in The Lotus Sutra describing the activities of this figure is one of the most popular pieces of all Mahayana writing. In some ways therefore the contents of these two writings are complementary and the manner of thinking summed up in the concept 'skilful means' emerges coherently from a study of them.

When it comes to The Perfection of Insight Sutras and the dependent literature, the criterion of frequency of use is not so clear. The outstandingly popular Diamond Sutra and Heart Sutra are very brief indeed and Kumārajīva's Chinese versions happen not to contain a single instance of the term under study, though they do need to be mentioned again later. Chapter Six below is based selectively on Kumārajīva's translations of the basic text of The Perfection of Insight Sutra, of the larger text in '25000' lines, and of the treatises mentioned above. It cannot be said that any of these are really popular. There is for example no Japanese rendering of these longer forms of the sutra, though there is of the shorter treatises.[18] Nevertheless the prin-

---

[18] *Kokuyaku Issaikyō*, series of Japanese translations first published in the 1920's and 1930's, recently reprinted, *Chūganbu* Vol. 1. See also Ui Hakuju: *Ui Hakaju Chosaku Senshū*, Vols. 4 & 5, Tokyo 1968, containing the three shorter treatises. The *Kokuyaku Issaikyō* also contains a translation of the great extended form of The Perfection of Insight Sutra (*Daihan-nyakyō*, or *Daihannyaharamittakyō*) which takes up no less than three volumes of the *Daizōkyō* in Chinese (T220). Presumably this work has had some influence, although for this class of literature one could almost formulate a law that the shorter it is, the greater its influence.

ciples of 'perfection of insight' thinking are widely current as a result of the general use of the shorter sutras and monastic use of the longer forms and the treatises. The term 'skilful means' itself is quite common in the longer texts and reflects the same usage as that found in The Lotus Sutra and The Teaching of Vimalakīrti. There is a particularly strong emphasis on the relationship between 'skilful means' and 'insight', and a discussion of this in Chapter Six follows on most conveniently from the usage in The Teaching of Vimalakīrti. In the same chapter some reference to the usage in the treatises establishes the links with Mādhyamika thought, which for Kumārajīva 'was simply Mahāyāna in śāstra form'.[19]

The idea of 'skilful means' does not lie buried in the texts mentioned above. If it is true that the texts represent in a general way the formative stage of Mahayana Buddhism as it was first conceived in India, even though the Chinese versions are at one remove from the originals, then general questions arise about the relationship between the Mahayana idea of 'skilful means' and pre-Mahayana Buddhism. These matters do not depend on minor questions of textual analysis (although a few come into it) but rather on an assessment of central characteristics of the Buddhist religion, and they are therefore raised in Chapter Seven below.

The texts studied have formed such staple reading and recitation material for later Mahayanists that the idea of 'skilful means' is relevant to many later Chinese and Japanese writings. It would take volumes to study in detail even the explicit usage of the term in all the later texts, let alone to unravel the implicit ramifications of its influence. However some attempt has been made in Chapter Eight to link up with contemporary Buddhism by a survey of modern Japanese usage. No doubt there will be about 100 million corrections.

Finally, when the meaning of 'skilful means' has been sufficiently clarified in the Buddhist context itself, a brief and of course quite unhistorical attempt is made to lift the discussion into the wider world. This is done (in Chapter Nine) partly to dissipate the sensation of being forever imprisoned in historical data, and partly because it is felt that the style of thought uncovered here is indeed relevant to ways of interpreting life other than the Buddhist one.

Problems of terminology

The phrase 'skilful means' has already been used here and there by western writers, but unfortunately it reflects a slightly confusing situation with respect to the underlying Sanskrit, Chinese and Japanese terms with which we are concerned. Even that famous interpreter D. T. Suzuki showed some hesitation over how to bring the concept across into English.[20] Although the literal translation of the plain Sanskrit term *upāya* would be just 'means' and

---

[19] Robinson, *op. cit.* p. 95.

[20] See *Outlines of Mahayana Buddhism*, (New York 1963, but first published in 1907) p. 64,

not 'skilful means', it is arguable that the best English to use in general discussion of the specifically Buddhist concept is 'skilful means'.[21] The case for this will now be presented forthwith, partly as a natural prolegomenon, and partly because it contributes to the overall development of the topic.

There is an ordinary Sanskrit word: *upāya*, which means 'means', 'expedient', 'stratagem' and the like.[22] The straightforwardly secular meaning of the term can be judged from the enumeration of four such 'means' of success against an enemy, namely: sowing dissension, chastisement, conciliation, and

'The term *upāya* literally means expediency. The great fatherly sympathetic heart of the Bodhisattva has inexhaustible resources at his command in order that he might lead the masses to enlightenment . . . To reach this end he employs innumerable means (*upāya*) suggested by his disinterested lovingkindness'. Ibid. p. 260 f. (footnote): (after comparison with 1 Cor. XIII 2 and quotation from The Lotus Sutra) 'Upāya is a very difficult term to translate into English; it literally means "way", "method", or "strategy".' Ibid. p. 298 f. 'Upāya, meaning "expedient", "stratagem", or "device", or "craft", has a technical sense in Buddhism. It is used in contrast to intelligence (*prajñā*) and is synonymous with love (*karuṇā*). Suzuki then quotes from The Teaching of Vimalakīrti to indicate the connection with *prajñā* (the text appears later below), and gives a very generalised account of the concept typical of the style of *Outlines of Mahayana Buddhism*. He goes on: 'In many cases, thus, it is extremely difficult to render upāya by any of its English equivalents and yet to retain its original technical sense unsuffered. This is also the case with many other Buddhist terms, among which we mention Bodhi, Dharmakāya, Prajñā, Citta, Parivarta, etc. The Chinese translators have *fang p'ien* (*sic*) for upāya which means "means-accommodation".' The miscellaneous use of diacritical marks, italics and capital letters in these quotations illustrates the messy process of anglicising Buddhist terms quite well. In general one may concur with the intention not to be happy with a common English word which fails to do justice to the special meaning of *upāya* or *fang-pien* in Buddhism. Note also that 'insight' and 'compassion' are adequate for *prajñā* and *karuṇā*, and better than 'intelligence' and 'love' which are not adequate. The question of analogies to skilful means outside Buddhism will be taken up again briefly in Chapter Nine below.

[21] The Matsunagas, in the article previously noted (see note 2), say ' "skilful means" is aoristic without further elucidation' (*op. cit.* p. 51), but then go on to use regularly the word *upāya* itself, which is of course equally 'aoristic without further elucidation'. The significance of the concept can admittedly only be made clear by looking into it at some length, whether we speak of *upāya* (and leave *upāya-kauśalya* out of it altogether) or whether we speak of 'skilful means' to preserve the relevant associations. It is presumably because it needs some elucidation anyway that people have begun to write about it. It is also misleading to equate *upāya* entirely with *fang-pien*, in view of Kumārajīva's conflations with *upāya-kauśalya* (see below). Moreover, it is remarkable that the article does not seem to contain any further reference to 'skill' at all. The general intention to stick to the word *upāya* seems to break down on page 70, where they are described as 'methods', and Lu K'uan Yü's translation (of *fang-pien*) as 'expedient method' is accepted without comment in a quotation from The Teaching of Vimalakīrti. It is also argued that 'such renditions (i.e. "expediency", "adapted teaching" and "skilful means") imply that *upāya* are inferior teachings bearing only a marginal relationship to Buddhist philosophy' (page 51), a view rejected in the present work.

[22] Monier-Williams, *Sanskrit-English Dictionary*, Oxford 1899, gives: 'coming near, approach, arrival, Bhartr; that by which one reaches one's aim, a means or expedient (of any kind), way, stratagem, craft, artifice,' and locates this usage in the *Mahābhārata*, *Laws of Manu*, *Yājñavalkya* and *Pañcatantra*. H. Grassmann's *Wörterbuch zum Rig-veda*, Leipzig 1873, does not contain the term at all. Monier-Williams presumably consulted Böhtlingk and Roth's *Sanskrit-Wörterbuch* St. Petersburg 1855, Vol. I, p. 988 which gives: 'Herbeikunft, wodurch man zu seinem Ziel gelangt, Mittel, Weg, fein angelegtes Mittel'. References here are

gifts.[23] An example of the quite ordinary use of the term may be found in the *Hitopadeśa*. In the tenth fable of Chapter IV, The Brahman and his Goat, the term is used of a trick devised by three robbers who managed to deprive a Brahman of a goat which he had bought for sacrifice. They simply asked him whether he was sure it was not a dog (which would count as unclean and quite unsuitable for sacrifice) and continued to ask him this until he became quite unsure of himself and finally abandoned the animal by the roadside.[24]

Needless to say this is far from being the same as the Buddhist usage, which is controlled by other central Buddhist concepts. In passing it is curious to note that the air of disreputability which has sometimes become associated with the Japanese equivalent, *hōben*, has a parallel already in the usage of the Sanskrit term. If there were an extensive living 'Sanskrit' Buddhism today its representatives would presumably have to make use of the same kind of arguments in this connection as Japanese scholars and apologists employ (considered in Chapter Eight below).

The Sanskrit word *upāya* also has, of course, a purely etymological history, and some writers have attempted to draw out the meaning of the word from the verb *upa√i*, meaning: to approach, to arrive at, etc.[25] However it seems quite inappropriate to draw conclusions for Buddhist doctrine from such a remote etymological basis, even if there is some general continuity of meaning. Not only does the ordinary meaning of 'means' or 'device' far outweigh any such considerations as a prolegomenon for considering the Buddhist meaning, but beyond this the Buddhist meaning itself must be

wider than in Monier-Williams and include *Muṇḍakopanishad* 3, 2.4 and *Bhagavad-gītā* 6, 36. The last mentioned is in fact an explicitly religious usage, though one which naturally arises without becoming a technical term, to the effect that yoga can be attained by one who is self-controlled and who strives by means (*upāyataḥ*), that is, presumably, by appropriate means. The further exposition is not connected with this term in particular, and since it does not appear to be used otherwise in the text, it may be taken to be non-technical.

[23] Francis Johnson, *Hitopadeśa: The Sanskrit Text, with a Grammatical Analysis, Alphabetically Arranged*, London 1884, p. 146. He also gives two related terms: *upāya-chintā*, the devising of an expedient, and *upāya-jña*, skilled in expedients or fertile in resources. Monier-Williams also gives these terms; and the four means of success against an enemy as 'sowing dissension, negotiation, bribery, and open assault' which altogether add up to the same.

[24] Johnson, *Hitopadeśa*, p. 90 (of text), line 2542. cf. Charles Wilkins, *Fables and Proverbs from the Sanskrit, being the Hitopadesa*, London 1885, pp. 251-2 and 256. The eleventh fable in the same chapter (*ibid*, pp. 253-6) gives a story about a lion with three attendants, a crow, a tiger and a jackal. One day the lion decided to give protection to a wandering camel whom he also took into service. After some time the animals began to suffer from a food shortage, and the crow, the tiger and the jackal began to plot, and suggested to the lion that the camel be used for food. The lion objected since he had given his word that the camel should be protected. The three plotters then devised a stratagem by which the camel would be brought to offer himself voluntarily as food for the others. Each one of them in turn offered themselves to the lion as food, but the lion each time refused. In this way the camel was constrained not to lag behind, and he also offered himself, but when he did so he was immediately fallen upon and killed by the tiger. This second story is supposed to explain the same principle as the first one given above, namely that people may often be brought to grief by placing confidence in knaves.

[25] Kumoi, *op. cit.* pp. 324 ff. cf. also Sawada *op. cit.*

sought in the context of meaning provided by the fundamental Buddhist texts in which it is used.

There are a few occurrences of the term in the Pali Canon of Theravada Buddhism (and the Pali equivalent to the Sanskrit is, as it happens, exactly identical: *upāya*) but these are massively outnumbered by the usage in early Mahayana texts. Since the Pali usage is so limited it can be left aside until Chapter Seven below which considers the relationship between the Mahayana concept of skilful means and the general character of early Buddhism.

In the early Mahayana texts the term *upāya* became a technical term in its own right. For this reason it is listed, with examples, in Edgerton's *Buddhist Hybrid Sanskrit Dictionary*, although Edgerton does indicate, unusually, that it 'equals' Sanskrit.[26] Some compound formations are also to be found, the most important of these being *upāya-kauśalya* (Pali: *upāya-kosalla*), which means 'skill in means', 'skill in devices', etc. Edgerton gives the meaning of this compound as 'skill in expedients'. He also, rather surprisingly, quotes Kern's very antiquated interpretation from the Lotus Sutra, namely 'able management, diplomacy', which would be very free indeed as a translation, though acceptable as a preliminary suggestion.[27] Edgerton goes on to say that the term 'is extremely common everywhere' (i.e. in Buddhist Hybrid Sanskrit texts, which are almost entirely Mahayana), 'especially of the Buddha's skill in devising means to impress and convert people'. The only other compound term listed in Edgerton's dictionary is *upāya-kuśala* (Pali: *upāya-kusala*), an adjective related to *upāya-kauśalya* and meaning 'skilful in expedients'. This term is very rare however and can be left aside.

So far then two main terms have been introduced, namely:

upāya = 'means', 'device', etc.
upāya-kauśalya = 'skill in means', 'skill in devices', etc.

Neither of these is a literal basis for the English expression 'skilful means'. What then is the justification for this latter? The first reason lies in the distance between the implication of the ordinary Sanskrit term *upāya* and

---

[26] Edgerton, Franklin, *Buddhist Hybrid Sanskrit Dictionary and Grammar*, New Haven, 1953, *ad loc.*

[27] In fact Kern mainly translated *upāyakauśalya* as 'skilfulness', rather ignoring the *upāya* component. In the note quoted by Edgerton he goes on to say that *upāya* means an expedient, and that it also denotes the energy of *prajñā*, 'the latter being Nature, otherwise called Māyā', Kern, *op. cit.*, p. 30. Kern's interpretations should now be regarded as entirely antiquated, especially comments such as (p. 30) 'From the atheistic point of view the possessor of *upāyakauśalya* can hardly be anything else but all-ruling Time; regarded from the theistic view he must be the Almighty Spirit.' Burnouf was more precise at an earlier date when he explained *upāya* as 'le moyen' and *upāyakauśalya* as 'l'habileté dans l'emploi des moyens', *op. cit.* p. 550.

the use of the same term, with all its associations, in Buddhist texts composed in Buddhist Hybrid Sanskrit.

None of the English words: 'means', 'device', 'expedient', etc. really does justice by itself to the meaning of the word *upāya* as a technical term in Mahayana Buddhism. Moreover these English words tend to suggest a lower degree of ethical responsibility than should fairly be ascribed to Mahayanists, even though there is admittedly a problem about the correlation of Mahayanist ethics and western approaches to ethics. One of the overall conclusions of the investigation to be reported later below is that it would be misleading to speak of *upāya* in a Buddhist sense as 'just a means' or 'just a device', with a strongly pejorative suggestion of deviousness. Indeed consistency with respect to the use of rather diverse means is precisely one of the claims maintained in The Lotus Sutra, as will be seen. For this reason, whatever the conclusions of an independent observer may be, it seems desirable to find a phrase for Buddhist *upāya* which does not tend to suggest a meaning which Buddhists themselves argue to be misleading. Above all a Buddhist *upāya* is something created on the responsibility of a Buddha or a bodhisattva who has perfected his 'skill in means' (*upāya-kauśalya*). Since a Buddhist *upāya* is above all something to be skilfully devised and applied it seems natural to draw in this idea of skill in order to characterise the specifically Buddhist concept. Hence it seems right to speak of Buddhist *upāya* as 'skilful means'. This is not so colourless as mere 'means' and is sufficiently curious to act as a distinct technical term, in a manner which nevertheless remains quite appropriate to the original texts in which it is used. Of course translations of Mahayana texts in Buddhist Hybrid Sanskrit may want to follow the vocabulary more closely and use simply 'means' or 'expedient' for *upāya*. Translations have the advantage of a massive co-determining context. 'Skilful means' is proposed for use in discussion. The procedure here may seem to be rather bold to some. Curiously enough it finds significant further support in the Sino-Japanese Buddhist tradition.

The most usual Chinese term for *upāya* is *fang-pien* 方便 , the characters for which are pronounced in Japanese as *hō-ben*. (Characters for all Chinese and Japanese terms are given in the index.) In a sense the Chinese and Japanese words *fang-pien* and *hōben* are the same. They *look* the same in their written form. This does not mean however that they are really quite the same in language history. The Chinese word, like the Sanskrit word *upāya*, is an ordinary word meaning 'method', or 'convenient' etc.[28] It had an independent existence apart from its use by the translators of Buddhist texts. The Japanese word *hōben* however, since it is drawn from the Chinese, could not possibly have had any existence prior to the importation of Chinese culture to Japan, which was inextricably bound up with Buddhism and

---

[28] Giles, H. A. *Chinese-English Dictionary*, 1912, 1964, ad loc. gives rather crudely: 'convenient; the "good works" of Buddhism', plus some locutions stressing convenience or accommodation, e.g. 'If you are accommodating to others, you will find it an accommodation to yourself'. *Hsing fang-pien* (行方便) is given as 'to bestow alms, etc.' These all rather suggest that Chinese usage did not reflect the profounder aspects of Buddhist philosophy by the

Buddhist texts. Unlike the Chinese therefore it is in large measure a technical term from the beginning, though it did not entirely remain so.

Those who translated the Mahayana sutras into Chinese do not seem to have been very much concerned about the distinction between *upāya* and *upāya-kauśalya*. Dharmarakṣa, who composed the earliest extant Chinese version of The Lotus Sutra, favoured the term *shan-chüan fang-pien*,[29] while Kumārajīva preferred either just *fang-pien* or sometimes *fang-pien-li*.[30] In the texts studied Kumārajīva *never* used Dharmarakṣa's phrase, probably because he felt his own translation to be more succint. Some justification for Kumārajīva's tendency to compression may be seen in the way in which the two related terms are used in the Sanskrit text. There too the distinction is not in practice very important. Since either term immediately evokes the other the persistent reader would tend to conflate them in his mind. Striking confirmation of this point is found in the fact that Kumārajīva was able to translate the title of the second chapter of The Lotus Sutra from *upāya-kauśalya* to *fang-pien*, even though the latter, considered pedantically, is equivalent only to *upāya*.[31] Thus when Kumārajīva said *fang-pien* he meant 'means (such as buddhas skilfully use)'. The same applies for *fang-pien* as a facility of bodhisattvas, as when it is said in Kumārajīva's translation of The Great Perfection of Insight Sutra (T223): 'If a bodhisattva, a *mahāsattva*, desires to attain supreme perfect enlightenment, he should learn the perfec-

---

early twentieth century, although one further interesting phrase is 佛以慈悲爲本，方便爲門 interpreted as 'Buddha makes compassion the root and charity the door,—of salvation'. Mathews' *Chinese-English Dictionary*, Cambridge Mass. 1969 gives a few phrases following Giles, and for the term *fang-pien* itself writes as follows: 'convenient, from 隨方因便 that which is not strictly according to rule, but which is convenient. Used by Buddhists for good works, by means of which men are led into an appreciation of the deeper truths of Buddhist philosophy; now used generally of things beneficial.' The pocket-sized *Xīnhuá Zìdiǎn*, Peking 1971, does not use the term in the context of *fang* (方) or *fa* (法), but does use it to explain the meaning of *biàn* (便 i.e. *pien*) as 'convenient'. Sino-Japanese dictionaries are discussed in Chapter Eight below.

[29] 善權方便, frequently (see Appendix C). Suzuki translated this term as 'skilful means', *Studies in the Lankavatara Sutra*, p. 393.

[30] 方便 or 方便力. See Appendix C.

[31] Wogihara, U. and Tsuchida, C. do not indicate any alternative manuscript readings for this, *Saddharmapuṇḍarīka-sūtram, Romanized and Revised Text of the Bibliotheca Buddhica Publication*, Tokyo, 1934, p. 28, though the point may be subject to correction. Nor does N. Dutt in his *Saddharmapuṇḍarīkasūtram with N. D. Mironov's Readings from Central Asian Mss.*, Calcutta 1953. Anyway this is by no means the only case, for the next two occurrences in the text illustrate the point equally well. It is most unlikely that Kumārajīva's manuscript gave *upāya* in all such cases. The footnote to this heading in KSS explicitly equates *fang-pien* and *upāya-kauśalya*, perhaps simply presuming that Kumārajīva's is a correct translation of a Sanskrit like that now extant; the meaning is then given as 'appropriate expedient or tactful method', which shows the force of -*kauśalya* is not clearly appreciated. The translation of the chapter heading itself in KSS is 'Tactfulness', which is a good word for conveying an approximately correct impression without further explanations, but which does not really cover the sense of active, inventive, initiative demanded to cover the whole teaching activity of a Buddha. Kern translates this chapter heading merely as 'Skilfulness', and this is in-adequate because there is no good reason for ignoring the *upāya*- element in the Sanskrit.

tion of insight applying skilful means.'[32] Although the text literally says *fang-pien* it is evidently concise for '(while) applying (his) (skilfulness in) means'. Not the application of one particular device is meant here but the bringing to bear of the bodhisattva's special skill in means with respect to all particular means.

The Japanese word *hōben* (for *fang-pien*) is the only one of the various possibilities in Japanese which became established in really ordinary use. Numerous other synonyms may be offered (no less than fourteen in a modern Sanskrit-Japanese dictionary)[33] but these are only explanatory. Not only was the term *hōben* a technical term from the start, as mentioned above, it was also firmly established in Kumārajīva's sense because of the paramount influence of his translations by the time Buddhism came to Japan. Above all it was the concentrated usage in The Lotus Sutra and The Teaching of Vimalakīrti which gave its meaning for the Japanese. These two texts have been well-known and popular in Japan ever since the earliest period when they were associated with the seventh century Prince Shōtoku, the first Japanese national patron of Buddhism. Japanese scholars may have been aware of the wider usage of the word *fang-pien* in Chinese literature, as they are today, but the average Japanese was not. Moreover popular misuse of the term must post-date its introduction into the language and therefore some weight should be given to the Buddhist attempts to retrieve and maintain its properly Buddhist meaning (described in Chapter Eight). Thus from the Japanese point of view there is something to be said for giving the term a slightly special translation in English, and for not being satisfied with the weak generality of 'means' or 'device'. Indeed Japanese dictionaries sometimes define the meaning of *hōben* as *kōmyō na shudan*, which means precisely 'skilful means'.[34] Similarly the term *zengon*, the *zengon* of Dharmarakṣa's *zengonhōben* (Ch. *shan-chüan fang-pien*), is defined in a major Japanese dictionary of Buddhist terms as 'a skilful means' (*zengyō no gonbō*) and as 'having the same meaning as *hōben*'.[35] Thus the case for translating *hōben*, in even faintly Buddhist contexts, with the special phrase 'skilful means' is quite strong, and reinforces the decision to translate Kumārajīva's *fang-pien* in this way.

Dharmarakṣa only had the *shan-chüan* (clever expedients) of *shan-chüan-fang-pien* (善權方便) at this point (T IX 67c), but this is probably an abbreviation for his own longer term.

[32] 若菩薩摩訶薩欲得阿耨多羅三藐三藐菩提應方便學般若波羅蜜迴向 T VIII 345a.

[33] Ogiwara Unrai, *Bonwa Jiten* (荻原雲來，梵和辞典), cited *ad loc.* by Kumoi (*op. cit.* p. 324, gives the following terms for *upāya:* 接近，到着，手段，方策，工夫，策略，技巧[漢訳]方便，方計，巧便，権，権方便，如法，因縁，因縁方便。

[34] 巧妙な手段 cf. Chapter Nine below on 'Spectrum of usage in dictionary entries', and cf. also Chapter Two, note 3.

[35] Oda, et al. *Bukkyō Daijiten*, Tokyo 1954, 1972 (織田得能，佛教大辭典) (p. 1059, 善巧の權謀，方便と言ふ如し).

The overall situation can be set out in tabular form as follows:

	pre-Buddhist meaning	Buddhist meaning	post-Buddhist meaning
Sanskrit:	means, trick	means (but c.f. skill in means)	(ordinary meaning continues)
Chinese: *fang-pien*	method, convenient	(skilfully applied) means *or* skilful means	(ordinary meaning continues)
Japanese: *hōben*		skilful means	trick
English:		skilful means	

As for terms not included in the table, *upāya-kauśalya* should be repre-sented in English by 'skill in means', and Kumārajīva's *fang-pien-li* as 'power of skilful means'.[36] In line by line discussion or literalistic translation of Sanskrit texts 'means' or 'expedient' may be demanded for *upāya* to distinguish it sharply from *upāya-kauśalya*, which explicitly *adds* the idea of skill to that of means. This literalism however, though not without uses on occasion, runs the very real danger of failing to bring out the important specificity of the term *upāya* as a *Buddhist* term. It also ignores the tendency of the *kauśalya* component to become inseparable from *upāya* in Buddhist usage, a development which culminates in Kumārajīva's equation of the two. The best term for Kumārajīva's *fang-pien* is 'skilful means'. Granted the general coherence of the Sanskrit and the Sino-Japanese tradition, the best term for the concept in general discussions of Buddhism seems also to be 'skilful means'. This special term can still be distinguished from 'skill in means' when necessary, but it brings in both the necessary associations in a convenient way for general purposes.

---

[36] This term (方便力) really lies between 'skill in means' which he had before him, and 'power of means' which seems a little too vague. If 'skilful means' is acceptable for Kumārā-jīva's *fang-pien*, then 'power of skilful means' follows on naturally for *fang-pien-li*. But it should always be remembered that the inclusion of the 'skilful' component depends on understanding Kumarajiva's terms in their overall Buddhist context from the Sanskrit texts to contemporary Japanese explanations, rather than on translating it as if it were just a miscellaneous Chinese word.

2 THE INITIAL TEACHING OF SKILFUL MEANS IN THE LOTUS SUTRA

Śāriputra's perplexity

Taken as a unified text The Lotus Sutra seems on the face of it to offer a mysterious new doctrine heralded by fantastic celestial events. Indeed the elaborate description of the scenario, with a magisterial Buddha deep in meditation on the Vulture Peak, surrounded by a fantastic throng of *arhats* and bodhisattvas, not to mention the dragon-kings and others not often seen nowadays, makes tedious reading for some fast-moving moderns. The mythology will be taken up again below, but for the present immediate attention may be paid to the second chapter of the sutra where its main teaching is first directly stated. Other chapters of the sutra contain elaborations of the same teaching, partly in the form of allegories which will also be considered later including such famous tales as the burning house and the magic city.

In the Sino-Japanese tradition this second chapter has always had a special importance as the key to the understanding of the sutra as a whole. Usually it is coupled with Chapter XVI (Chapter 15 in Sanskrit texts)[1] which is given a final supremacy as the revelation of the true character of the Buddha. Given this standpoint of interpretation, which goes back to Chih-I, these two chapters have often been singled out for special liturgical use.[2] The doctrinal schematisations of this sort are not adopted here as a methodological basis. For one thing it is most likely that Chapter XVI (or 15) was not part of the earliest phase of the sutra's compilation, but even when the sutra was taken as a literary whole by Kumārajīva, the complex exegetical structures developed later were not as far as we know employed by him. Nevertheless, even leaving the doctrinal schemes aside, it is clear that Chapter II dominates the first part of the sutra, if not all of it. It has already been noted that Kumārajīva's title for it is precisely 'Skilful Means' (*fang-pien*).

---

[1] A synoptic table of chapters is given in Appendix B. Chapters for Sanskrit are always given in Arabic numbers because of their common origin, and chapters in the Chinese versions are always given with Roman numerals because of their accidental similarities with Chinese numerals.

[2] On Chih-I see general works such as K.K.S. Ch'en's *Buddhism in China A Historical Survey*, Princeton 1972, but especially L. Hurvitz: *Chih-I (538-597) An Introduction to the Life and Ideas of a Chinese Buddhist Monk*, Brussels 1962, (*Mélanges Chinois et Bouddhiques* XII 1960-62). Some Japanese writers continue to give the dogmatic pattern for reference (*nimon-rokudan* 二門六段 i.e. two gates and six stages), as for example Ōchō Keinichi in *Hokkekyō Josetsu,* 法華経序説 Kyoto 1962 and 1972, pp. 116-7. However it would be a complete mistake to think that Japanese studies of The Lotus Sutra are always controlled by this idea, as western pandits sometimes assert. On the contrary, Japanese scholarship *per se* entirely accepts the historical perspective, although the traditional exegesis not unnaturally lingers in the religious world.

The narrative framework is quite simple. Following on from the preparatory explanation in the opening chapter the Buddha rises from his contemplation and briefly explains to Śāriputra and the whole assembly the relation between the insight of the buddhas and their style of teaching. The audience, including Śāriputra who was supposed to be one of the wisest of his disciples,[3] fails to understand his meaning, and so Śāriputra, as spokesman, requests a further explanation. At first the Buddha demurs on the grounds that it would merely startle and perplex people, but when the request is repeated twice more he agrees to speak. At this point five thousand haughty members of the audience withdraw, believing that they have already attained what there is to attain, and then the Buddha begins again to expound at some length the doctrine of skilful means.

The theme is already briefly anticipated in the description of the heart-searching of the audience, and in Śāriputra's first request, although it does not appear in the repetitions of the request which stress instead the willingness of large numbers of the audience to hear a fuller exposition with respect. The perplexity of the audience has three aspects. Firstly, why does the Buddha now so earnestly praise the practice of skilful means?[4] Secondly, why does he say that the Dharma which he has obtained is so profound and difficult to understand?[5] Thirdly, what does this mean with regard to the one principle of emancipation leading to Nirvana, which has already been declared, and which is followed by monks, nuns, and lay devotees both male and female who seek to become *śrāvakas* and *pratyekabuddhas*?[6]

In Śāriputra's request for further elucidation 'the supreme skilful means'[7]

---

[3] T IX 6b 'Although the Buddha says that I am the first in all this assembly of disciples (i.e. *śrāvakas*), now in my own wisdom I am in doubt and cannot understand: is this the final limit of Dharma or is it the way to progress there?' (於諸聲聞衆　佛說我第一　我今自於智 疑惑不能了　爲是究竟法　爲是所行道) cf. KSS 39f. Śāriputra is traditionally supposed to have been converted along with Maudgalyāyana and five hundred followers after an encounter with one of the original five hermits converted by the Buddha. He frequently appears in dialogues with the Buddha to represent the Hinayana standpoint in Mahayana writings. In The Teaching of Vimalakīrti he is made to seem rather foolish, worrying over where the assembly will sit down in Vimalakīrti's magically emptied room (Chapter VI) and being temporarily turned into a female by a goddess to whom he was rash enough to suggest that she might be better off as a male (Chapter VII).

[4] T IX 6b 何故慇懃稱歎方便 cf. KSS 38.

[5] T IX 6b 佛所得法甚深難解 cf. KSS 38.

[6] T IX 6b 佛說一解脫義。我等亦得此法到於涅槃。而今不知是義所趣 'The Buddha has declared one principle of release and we too on receiving this Dharma can attain nirvana. But now we do not know what this principle implies.' Cf. KSS 38.

[7] T IX 6b 第一方便 cf. KSS 38. 'Skilful means' is used here throughout. 'Tactful method', which is usually given in KSS, though very suggestive, does not quite cover the idea of skill sufficiently, though of course tact does involve skill. For The Lotus Sutra alone 'tactful method' would probably do, for the tactfulness is mainly that of the Buddha towards all sentient beings. More generally it is not so adequate, for the bodhisattva needs to practice and perfect this skill to maintain his balancing act between nirvana and the salvation of others without fear; in such cases it really is 'skill' and not 'tact' which is required.

is again closely identified with the Dharma itself, and both are spoken of as the property of all the buddhas. Thus he asks: 'What is the cause and what the reason for so earnestly extolling the supreme skilful means and the very profound, mysterious Dharma of the buddhas, which is so difficult to understand?'[8] Reference to the skilful means and Dharma of buddhas in general is of some importance.[9] By contrast Śāriputra goes on to say, 'From of yore I have never heard such a discourse from the Buddha',[10] but this latter statement refers only to Śāriputra's experience of the present Buddha, and does not indicate the overall standpoint of the sutra. Similarly the audience as a whole was perplexed because hitherto only one principle of emancipation has been declared, namely the teaching of Nirvana, which they have already received. To the audience, including Śāriputra, a new teaching seems to be in the offing, but from the overall standpoint of the sutra's teaching the 'new' teaching is simply the teaching of all buddhas in all times and places. The newness is felt by the recipients of the teaching because it is they who differentiate and make progress. From the standpoint of 'the buddhas' however the apparently varied teaching is quite consistent. The effects of this dialectic upon the way in which traditional concepts of Buddhism are understood will be brought out in more detail below, but before going further something should be said about the sense in which the teaching of this sutra is supposed to be 'new'.

It is clear from the formulations already referred to and quoted that the very theme of the Buddha's discourse in The Lotus Sutra is supposed to be his skilful means, which is intimately connected with his Dharma and which he shares in common with all the buddhas. Apart from this theme there is indeed no particular 'content' to the teaching given. It is a sutra therefore not so much about doctrines in an assertive sense, but rather about the inner method of the Buddhist religion. For example there is little concern about whether there is an attainable goal, Nirvana, or not, but there is much concern about the whys and wherefores of such a goal being held out for people to entertain and about what they should do with it. As the questioners referred to above put it: 'We too on receiving this Dharma attain Nirvana. *But now we do not know to what this principle tends*'.[11] The sutra is about the correct use of existing religious procedures. It does not propose the setting up of new religious procedures, though it perhaps encourages a certain widening of outlook with regard to permissible accessories (see below). Since it is about a religious *method* it is not a speculative writing but an extremely practical, spiritual one. It is not about doctrines in the pedestrian sense that it sets out

---

[8] T IX 6b 何因何緣慇懃稱歎諸佛第一方便。甚深微妙難解之法。Cf. KSS 38.

[9] In Sanskrit the buddhas are tathāgatas (upāya-kauśalyam *tathāgatānāṃ*, and then ta thāgatānām *upāya-kauśalya* . . . Wogihara and Tsuchida, *op. cit.* p. 32. The Chinese 諸佛 (equivalent to 'buddhas') used here is just an indication of the complete synonymity of these terms.

[10] T IX 6b 我自昔來未曾從佛聞如是說 cf. KSS 38.

[11] Or 'what this principle implies', see text and translation in note 6 above. Italics are of course added.

a series of doctrines for memorisation or assent. There are no new teachings as such which could be straightforwardly enumerated. Hence the reaction of some, on a first reading, that the much heralded 'new' revelation of the Buddha never amounts to anything much. Nevertheless, although there is no new 'content', what does emerge is a controversial new style for understanding the existing teaching, and in this sense the sutra is indeed about doctrine. This new style, which touches the very centre of what Buddhism is all about, is inextricably bound up with the elaboration of the notion of skilful means as that which above all characterises the observable activity of a buddha.

The material giving the Buddha's exposition can be considered in three parts: the brief opening exposition which was not understood by the audience, the longer exposition in prose, and the longer exposition in verse. It may be recollected that the intention is to bring out the meaning of 'skilful means' as it stands in Kumārajīva's Chinese version, and thus there is no impropriety in looking first at the prose sections even though historically it may be that the verse, or some of it, was composed at an earlier date.

The opening exposition

Not surprisingly the brief opening exposition contains essentially the same three points of interest as the question of Śāriputra already commented upon, namely: the wisdom or insight of the buddhas, their method or means, and the question about how what is said about these relates to existing Buddhist teaching. Great emphasis is placed on the perfection of the buddhas, with regard to insight and skilful means, thus: 'The *tathāgatas* are all already completely perfect in the *pāramitās* of skilful means and wisdom.'[12] The insight of a buddha or a *tathāgata* (these are of course more or less interchangeable terms) is said to be quite superlative and not shared by any other beings at all.[13] Their Dharma is 'faultless and inscrutable, profound and mysterious'.[14] It 'cannot be indicated' and 'the terms for it are characterised by nirvana'.[15] Their insight is 'broad and great, profound and far-reaching'.[16] But while being inexpressible it also involves a grasp of the true nature of the multiple factors of existence.

This latter aspect of the Buddha's insight found a clearly formalised expression in Kumārajīva's version when he wrote: 'Only a buddha together

---

[12] T IX 5c 如來方便知見波羅蜜皆已具足 Cf. KSS 32, but *pāramitā* surely goes with skilful means as well as with wisdom; and the plural seems to be required for 如來 (cf. also plural forms throughout this context in the Sanskrit). Wisdom here is 知 and 見, i.e. *jñāna-darśana*, but may be taken as a synonym of 智慧 (*prajñā*).

[13] The verse shortly after says that bodhisattvas are an exception (除諸菩薩眾 T IX 5c cf. KSS 35).

[14] T IX 6a 無漏不思議甚深微妙法 cf. KSS 37.

[15] T IX 5c 是法不可示，言辭相寂滅 cf. KSS 35: 'This Law is inexpressible, it is beyond the realm of terms;'

[16] T IX 5c 如來知見廣大深遠 cf. KSS 32-3.

with a buddha can fathom the true nature of all dharmas: that all dharmas have such a form, such a nature, such an embodiment, such a potency, such a function, such a primary cause, such a secondary cause, such an effect, such a recompense, and such a complete fundamental whole.'[17] This list of the ten 'suchnesses' is not found *in toto* in any extant Sanskrit and it may be that Kumārajīva was improving on the text before him at this point.[18] Nevertheless the passage represents a rounding up of what is in principle also present in the Sanskrit and the author or authors of the latter were certainly also implying that recognition of the true character of all dharmas, that is of the multiple factors of existence, belongs to the stuff of buddhahood. The ten categories as formalised by Kumārajīva became an important list in the T'ien T'ai school of Buddhism because the founder of that school, Chih-I, used it as a basis for his famous phrase *I-nien san-ch'ien*, (J. *Ichinen sanzen*) meaning 'three thousand (worlds) in one thought'.[19] The main point of this formulation, which has been pondered and commented on down the centuries in the Sino-Japanese tradition, seems to have lain in a perfect, unitive, inner grasp of the real nature of all the diverse factors of existence.

The passage from the sutra quoted immediately above, whatever its precise pedigree may have been, is by no means out of character with the text as a whole. Indeed the same passage states that the various attainments of the Buddha enable him 'to enter deeply into the boundless and to accomplish all the unprecedented Dharma', and then goes on to say, 'The *Tathāgata* is able to discriminate everything, expound the dharmas skilfully, use gentle words and cheer up the hearts of all.'[20] As if to reinforce the juxtaposition the next sentence reasserts that 'Essentially speaking, the Buddha has altogether accomplished the infinite, boundless, unprecedented Dharma.'[21] Thus it *belongs* to the unitive insight of the *Tathāgata* that he is able to discriminate in a soteriologically effective way.

This double character of the Buddha's insight, its profundity and inaccessibility together with its formulation in teachings appropriate for releasing living beings from their attachment to this or that, is found also in the very first paragraph of this chapter of the sutra, which may now be quoted in full.

'The insight of the buddhas is very profound and infinite. Their school of insight is difficult to understand and difficult to enter, so that the *śrāvakas* and *pratyekabuddhas* cannot apprehend it. What is the reason for this? The

[17] T IX 5c 唯佛與佛乃能究盡諸法實相。所謂諸法如是相。如是性。如是體。如是力。如是作。如是因。如是緣。如是果。如是報。如是本末究竟等。cf. KSS 33-4. The latter gives 諸法 as 'All Existence', and 'dharmas' is only preferred here because it refers to the whole business of dharma-theory as this has become known to western students of Buddhism. Dharmas are factors of existence.

[18] The Sanskrit is presumably not satisfactorily rendered by Kern, *ad loc.* Cf. a discussion of the whole matter in Hurvitz, *op. cit.* pp. 271 ff.

[19] 一念三千 Chih-I had a special way of calculating to this number, see Hurvitz, *op. cit.* p. 311.

[20] T IX 5c 如來能種種分別巧說諸法。言辭柔軟悅可衆心。cf. KSS 33.

[21] T IX 5c 取要言之。無量無邊未曾有法。cf. KSS 33.

buddhas have been in fellowship with countless hundreds of thousands of myriads of *koṭis* of buddhas, perfectly practicing the infinite Dharma of all buddhas, boldly and zealously advancing, making their fame universally known, perfecting the very profound unprecedented Dharma, and expounding as opportunity served its meaning which is so difficult to understand. Śāriputra! Ever since I became Buddha I have widely discoursed and taught with various karmic reasonings and various parables, and I have led living beings to the abandonment of all attachments with innumerable skilful means. What is the reason for this? The *tathāgatas* are all already completely perfected in the *pāramitās* of means and insight.'[22] Thus these first two points are inextricable from each other.

The reference to *śrāvakas* and *pratyekabuddhas* here raises the third point to be noted, namely the problem about how what is said in this sutra relates to existing Buddhist teaching. (*Śrāvakas* are 'hearers' or disciples of the Buddha, while *pratyekabuddhas* attain enlightenment alone and do not proclaim it.) From the point of view of The Lotus Sutra itself that which the Buddha knows and the manner in which he teaches is something which he shares with innumerable buddhas. The problem, in so far as there is one, is that of the newness sensed by recipients of the skilfully differentiated teaching. It is a problem which only arises *within* the teaching activity of a single buddha. The *śrāvakas* and *pratyekabuddhas* are presented as not appreciating the full context or the full implications of that to which they are attaining. They do not understand it, according to the paragraph quoted above, because it is too difficult to understand *and because* the Buddha uses skilful means! By the very nature of the case such methods give rise to an appearance of inconsistency which is perplexing enough until their true intention is recognised. In order to benefit from the 'tactful methods' or skilful means of the Buddha it is necessary not only to make use of them as they are at first presented but also to discern in them *that towards which they tend*. In any given case there will be a crisis point at which the provisional character of the method is about to become apparent. The crisis involves an initial perplexity with regard to that which has hitherto been assumed, and this perplexity in turn issues either in a successful transcending of the device or in a haughty refusal to make further progress. These alternative attitudes are dramatised in the departure of the proud monks already described.

This third point also finds particularly clear expression in the verse form of the brief opening exposition. These are the verses in question.

'You should know, Śāriputra,
That there is no inconsistency in the words of the buddhas.
In the Dharma which the Buddha expounds

[22] T IX 5c 諸佛智慧甚深無量。其智慧門難解難入。一切聲聞辟支佛所不能知。所以者何。佛曾親近百千萬億無數諸佛。盡行諸佛無量道法。勇猛精進名稱普聞。成就甚深未曾有法。隨宜所說意趣難解。舍利弗。吾從成佛已來。種種因緣。種種譬喻。廣演言教。無數方便引導眾生。所以者何。如來方便知見波羅蜜。皆已具足。cf. KSS 32. In this case 'insight' or 'wisdom' (KSS) is *prajñā*, cf. note 12 above.

You should conceive a great power of faith.
Now that the World-honoured One has preached the Dharma for a long
    time
He must certainly proclaim the true reality.
To all the *śrāvakas*, and
To those seeking the vehicle of the *pratyekabuddhas*,
To those whom I have freed from the bondage of suffering
And who have reached nirvana,
I announce that the Buddha uses the power of skilful means
And points the way by teaching the three vehicles;
All beings have various attachments and
He leads them on to win their escape.'[23]

Here the very consistency of Buddhism has obviously been felt to be in question, and unless one has the insight of a Buddha oneself an act of faith is required to accept that there is a fundamental unity behind the various forms of teaching which are offered. Most important, the teaching of nirvana, which has been the inspiration of the *śrāvakas* and *pratyekabuddhas*, has to be recognised as being itself just one such form which, like all the others, has to be both used and transcended or superseded. There is no further definable point at which the means themselves are either affirmed or rejected. Rather the affirmation and the rejection belong together in so far as they tend to emancipation. Only the combination tends to emancipation.

The famous 'three' vehicles are referred to here. Though not specified by name, the third is the bodhisattva-vehicle, and like the others it must be understood as being differentiated in accordance with the Buddha's skilful means. This point will arise again below.

The longer exposition in prose

The second, and slightly longer exposition in this second chapter of the sutra pursues the same themes in greater detail, but with an important new emphasis on the oneness of the Buddha-vehicle.

As conveyed in the mythological parts of the sutra, a countlessly reflected procedure is carried on by the buddhas of the past, the future buddhas, the buddhas at present active in innumerable buddha-lands and the Buddha presently speaking in The Lotus Sutra. Contrary to the popular view of the

---

[23] T IX 6a 舍利弗當知　諸佛語無異　於佛所說法　當生大信力　世尊法久後　要當說
眞實　告諸 聲聞衆　及求緣覺乘　我令脫苦縛　逮得涅槃者　佛以方便力　示以三乘敎
衆生處處著　引之令得出 Cf. KSS 37 'True reality' (J. *shinjitsu*) is commonly contrasted with *hōben* in Japanese Buddhism, e.g. in the title of Kumoi's article quoted in Chapter One above, note 2. Sakamoto, *op. cit.* p. 349 declares that the teaching first given over a long period was a skilful means (*hōben* 方便) with which the true reality (*shin-jitsu* 眞實) may be contrasted. Remember however the earlier warning that this new or supreme teaching does not turn out to have 'content' in the same way as the earlier teaching had, but is no other than the declaration of the true character of the older teaching as skilful means.

buddhology of The Lotus Sutra the present Buddha does not claim to be a unique super-buddha, but says, 'Now I too am also like them' (i.e. like all the other buddhas).[24] Like the other buddhas he knows the condition of living beings and teaches them accordingly, thus: 'Knowing that all living beings have many kinds of desires deeply implanted in their minds, I expound the Dharma in accordance with their basic disposition by means of various karmic reasonings, similes, verbal expressions and my power of skilful means.'[25] In spite of the variety in the form of teaching however, 'The purpose of all of these is to secure perfect knowledge of the one Buddha-vehicle.'[26] The whole passage is very closely parallel to those which precede it about other buddhas, past and future, and in other worlds in space. They *all* use skilful means for the sake of the one Buddha-vehicle.

Again and again it is insisted that the variety of teachings is all for the sake of the one Buddha-vehicle. Whatever the buddhas do always has the same purpose, namely 'only to make the Buddha-knowledge clear to all living beings.'[27] Indeed, this is why they appear in the world at all. Stated a little more elaborately, 'The buddhas, the world-honoured ones, appear in the world only on account of one very great karmic cause',[28] and that is, variously stated, 'to cause all living beings to open buddha-knowledge and gain purity', 'to manifest Buddha-knowledge to all living beings', 'to cause all living beings to awaken to Buddha-knowledge' and 'to cause all living beings to enter the way of Buddha-knowledge'.[29] The meaning of the Dharma which the buddhas expound is 'difficult to understand' but it is expounded 'as opportunity serves' by means of the various devices already mentioned.[30] This is because the Dharma itself cannot be understood by ordinary discriminative thought but only by buddhas.[31] The variety of teaching is therefore on the side of the recipients while the buddhas have but a single purpose. Were it not for this great karmic cause they would not appear at all. As it is they appear rarely enough, just as the *udumbara* flower is seen only once in three thousand years.

It is in such a context that the tension between the various forms of the Buddha's teaching are to be understood. As before, the question is whether

[24] T IX 7b 我令亦復如是 cf. KSS 46.

[25] T IX 7b 和諸衆生有稚稚欲深心所著。隨其本性。以種種因緣譬喻言辭方便力而為說法。 cf. KSS 46. There does not seem to be any particular justification for a past tense.

[26] T IX 7b 如此皆為得一佛乘一切種智故 cf. KSS 46. Śāriputra's name is then repeated again here rather soon as if he is being pressed to take this point to heart.

[27] T IX 7b 唯以佛之知見示悟衆生 cf. KSS p. 44. 'Reveal' is perhaps a little misleading to some readers, suggesting a revelation of what was not yet there, whereas the Buddha knowledge has always been there for people to awaken to. Two characters here conflate the 'manifest' and the '(cause to) awaken to' of phrases quoted just below (cf. note 29).

[28] T IX 7a 諸佛世尊。唯以一大事因緣故出現於世。 cf. KSS 44. Or 'come out'; in Japanese ghosts are said to 'come out'.

[29] T IX 7a 欲令衆生開佛知見使得清淨故...欲示衆生佛之知見故...欲令衆生悟佛知見故...欲令衆生入佛知見道故 cf. KSS 44.

[30] T IX 7a 諸佛隨宜說法意趣難解 cf. KSS 43.

[31] T IX 7a 唯有諸佛乃能知之 cf. KSS 43.

the various forms are consistent. Apparent inconsistencies are seen by the unenlightened, but consistency belongs to the Buddha, the Enlightened. Thus it is part of the respect shown by the unenlightened towards the Buddha to *believe* that his teaching is consistently true and contains no admixture of falsehood. 'Śāriputra,' says the Buddha, 'believe me, all of you; in the Buddha's teaching no word is false.'[32] This sentiment is repeated in another place in a way which clearly links the question of consistency and credibility with the idea of the single Buddha-vehicle, thus: 'Śāriputra! You should, with all your heart, believe and discern, receive and keep the word of the Buddha. No word of the *buddha-tathāgatas* is false; there is no other vehicle, but only the one Buddha-vehicle.'[33]

It has already been pointed out that the variety of teachings is said to be necessary because of the condition of living beings who 'have many kinds of desires deeply implanted in their minds'.[34] This state of affairs can also be presented cosmologically, as in the section now being considered. In the ancient Indian thought-world, in terms of which the Buddhist sutras were composed, time is divided into periods (*kalpas*) during which physical universes first develop and then decay. According to The Lotus Sutra 'The buddhas appear in the evil ages of the five decays, that is to say, decay of the *kalpa*, decay through tribulations, decay of all living creatures, decay of views, and decay of lifetime.'[35] In such times 'all living beings are very vile, being covetous and envious, bringing to maturity every root of badness.'[36] At such times therefore 'the buddhas, by their power of skilful means, in the one Buddha-vehicle discriminate and expound the three'.[37] Clearly, it may be remarked, since the buddhas themselves expound the three they are not without value, and one could not be satisfied with an easy polemical preference for one of the three. The following sentence is crucial for the whole dialectic of the matter and runs 'If my disciples who call themselves *arhats* or *pratyekabuddhas* neither hear nor understand that the *buddha-tathāgatas* teach only bodhisattvas, these are not the Buddha's disciples nor *arhats* nor *pratyekabuddhas*.'[38] The idea that the buddhas teach only bodhisattvas is used to bring about the necessary critique of the other two vehicles, but the bodhisattva-vehicle itself is still on the side of the three, that is, it still belongs to discriminatory exposition. Therefore the bodhisattva-vehicle is also required to be transformed and superseded by the one Buddha-vehicle which gives an equal validity to the other two. All provisional vehicles must give way to the final intention of the teaching or they lose their value alto-

---

[32] T IX 7a 舍利弗。汝等當信佛之所說言不虛妄。cf. KSS 43.

[33] T IX 7c 舍利弗。汝等當一心信解受持佛語。諸佛如來言無虛妄。無有餘乘唯一佛乘。cf. KSS 48.

[34] See note 25.

[35] T IX 7b 諸佛出於五濁惡世。所謂劫濁煩惱濁衆生濁見濁命濁。cf. KSS 46-7.

[36] T IX 7b ...衆生垢重。慳貪嫉妒成就諸不善根故。cf. KSS 47.

[37] T IX 7b 諸佛以方便力於一佛乘分別說三。cf. KSS 47.

[38] T IX 7b 若我弟子。自謂阿羅漢辟支佛者。不聞不知諸佛如來但教化菩薩事。此非佛弟子。非阿羅漢。非辟支佛。cf. KSS 47.

gether. It is only by being dismantled that they come to fruition. It is in this sense that the polemical relationship between the Mahayana and early Buddhism is to be understood. It turns on the spiritual state of the disciples themselves. The Lotus Sutra continues, 'Again, Śāriputra! You should know that those monks and nuns who claim that they have already become *arhats* and say 'This is our last bodily state before final nirvana,' and thereupon do not again devote themselves to seek after supreme perfect enlightenment, are all extremely conceited.'[39] The statement has a polemical edge, just like the story of the five thousand proud members of the audience who left the assembly, and presumably it illustrates a historical rivalry within ancient Buddhism. Nevertheless the interesting thing is again the dialectic implied in the subsequent, explanatory sentence, which runs 'There is no such thing as a monk who has really attained *arhat*-ship if he has not believed this Dharma.'[40] It appears that 'really' attaining *arhat*-ship entails arriving at a recognition of the provisional and dispensable character of the attainment. It is the opposite of being conceitedly stuck. It involves a dialectical fluidity which allows a certain positive status to the means skilfully provided by the buddhas, for they are consistent; and which at the same time is not attached to these means, because the goal is indeed not the means but the supreme enlightenment of the buddhas themselves. This view of the matter is not at all a simple polemicism, as it involves neither the straightforward affirmation nor the straightforward rejection of the goal of *arhat*-ship as such. Rather it means that *arhat*-ship is appropriately used as a skilful means of the buddhas in so far as it is left behind to make way for the real. It is not ultimately a question of replacing one vehicle with another, as there is no other vehicle apart from the Buddha-vehicle. Nor should any mistake be made with regard to a supposed special position for the bodhisattva-vehicle, for 'In the whole universe there are not even two vehicles, how much less a third.'[41]

The longer exposition in verse (i)

This part of Chapter Two of The Lotus Sutra consists of just over one hundred verses. Historically speaking the underlying Sanskrit of these verses may of course contain older material than the prose parts of the passages

---

[39] T IX 7 b-c 又舍利弗。是諸比丘比丘尼。自謂已得阿羅漢是最後身究竟涅槃。便不復志求阿耨多羅 三藐三菩提。當知此輩皆是增上慢人。cf. KSS 47. 'Supreme perfect enlightenment' appears as a transliteration for *anuttara-samyak-sambodhi*.

[40] T IX 7c 若有比丘實得阿羅漢。若不信此法。無有是處。cf. KSS 47.

[41] T IX 7b 十方世界中尚無二乘，何況有三。cf. KSS 46. Cf. also T IX 8a 十方佛土中唯有一乘法　無二亦無三　除佛方便說 'In the buddha-lands of the ten directions there is only one vehicle of Dharma. There is no second and no third, except for the Buddha's exposition of skilful means.' The question of three vehicles and the relation of the third to the buddha-vehicle (sometimes seen as a fourth term and sometimes equated with the third) is a subject in itself. The position as stated here is thought to represent The Lotus Sutra accurately and briefly, but if some qualification were needed it would not affect the theory of skilful means particularly.

already considered, but as Kumārajīva's version stands they consolidate and elaborate the themes already set out. Three more or less distinct sections may be discerned, the middle one corresponding to verses 77-95 in the Sanskrit, which according to Rawlinson may represent a later stage in elaboration than the others.[42] However that may be it will be appropriate in any case to treat the three sections one by one as they now stand in the Chinese.

Less is said at this point about the profundity of the Buddha's insight, but his understanding of the condition of sentient beings is stressed at some length. For example,

> 'What they entertain in their minds,
> All the ways they practise,
> All their many different desires,
> And their former karma, good and evil,
> The Buddha knows all these perfectly.'[43]

A more painful description of the state of unenlightened beings is found a little later, when they are said to transmigrate without hope in the six states of existence and to be deeply attached to the sixty-two false views. The latter arise out of concern with questions of ontological status, 'whether things are, or whether they are not', which means incidentally that it is absurd to read The Lotus Sutra as a quasi-theistic form of Buddhism or as if it introduces a new and un-Buddhist ontology.[44] It is not just a question of views, but also of attitudes:

> 'Self-sufficient and self-inflated,
> Suspicious, crooked and faithless in mind . . .
> Men such as these are hard to save.'[45]

In view of this analysis of the condition of beings, the teaching of nirvana is given as a skilful means.

> 'For this reason, Śāriputra,
> I set up a skilful means for them,
> Expounding the way to end all sufferings,
> And showing it by nirvana.'[46]

Yet the teaching on nirvana, even while given, is also dramatically withdrawn.

---

[42] Rawlinson, A., Ph.D. thesis for the University of Lancaster. Similarly verses 37-40, which pick up the narrative about the exit of the conceited monks, are also said to be of a distinct type, but such matters are of no importance for the present discussion.

[43] T IX 7c 衆生心所念　種種所行道　若干諸欲性　先世善惡業　佛悉知是已　cf. KSS 49.

[44] T IX 8b 若有若無 cf. KSS 53. On this point cf. a clear statement by H. von Glasenapp in 'Der Buddha des "Lotus des guten Gesetzes" ', *Jahrbuch des Lindenmuseums*, Heidelberg 1951, pp. 158 f.

[45] T IX 8b 我慢自矜高　諂曲心不實...如是入難度 cf. KSS 54.

[46] T IX 8b 是故舍利弗　我爲設方便　説諸盡苦道　示之以涅槃 cf. KSS 54. To 'show' or to 'indicate' is sufficient for 示 .

> 'Though I proclaim nirvana,
> Yet it is not a real extinction,
> Because all dharmas from the very beginning
> Are always nirvanic in themselves.'[47]

That is to say, the discursive spelling out of nirvana as a goal to be contrasted with ordinary existence is only necessary because sentient beings do not realise that the basic quality of all existence is nirvanic to start with. If they did realise it they would begin to feel the teaching to be contradictory, and so indeed it would be, were it not that as a skilful means of the Buddha it has its own rationale which requires not only that it be established or set up[48] but also that it be reduced and finally made redundant.

The teaching of nirvana is of course a central teaching of early Buddhism and for this reason, in view of the way in which it is treated here, there is a continued emphasis on the relationship between the two, or three, vehicles and the one or great vehicle (*mahāyāna*). Sometimes three vehicles and sometimes two are contrasted with the one, but the upshot seems to be the same. Thus:

> 'I have the power of skilful means
> To manifest the Dharma in three vehicles;
> But all the world-honoured ones,
> All of them, expound the way of one vehicle.
> Now let all this great assembly
> Be free from doubts and perplexities.
> The buddhas do not differ in their statements,
> There is one only and no second vehicle.'[49]

Early Buddhism is also referred to here in terms of the classification of the teaching in nine divisions. The nine referred to are: sermons (*sūtra*), verses (*gāthā*), former things (*itivṛttaka*), birth-stories (*jātaka*), marvels (*adbhuta*), origins (*nidāna*), parables (*aupamya*), mingled prose and verse (*geya*) and expositions (*upadeśa*). The Chinese text partly transliterates and partly translates the Sanskrit terms given in brackets here.[50] Similar lists appear in

---

[47] T IX 8b 我雖說涅槃　是亦非眞滅　諸法從本來　常自寂滅相 cf. KSS 54. The first two lines are apparently absent in the Sanskrit, but they only prepare the way for the strong statement in the second two. This, and not some new quasi-monotheism, is the fundamental metaphysical position, if it is a position, of the sutra. This is such an important verse that Iwamoto's translation of the Sanskrit into current Japanese may be quoted as well: 一切のものは常に平安で最初かろ静かである i.e. 'all things are permanently at rest and peaceful (*shizuka*) from the beginning.' Sakamoto and Iwamoto, *op. cit.* Vol. I, p. 111. Cf. also note 78 below, quoting another formulation of this same idea.

[48] Cf. the stanzas just quoted, especially 設. A deliberate intention is implied.

[49] T IX 8b-c 我有方便力　開示三乘法　一切諸世尊　皆說一乘道　今此諸大衆　皆應除疑惑　諸佛語無異　唯一無二乘 cf. KSS 54. Cf. also note 41 above.

[50] T IX 7c 或說修多羅　伽陀及本事　本生未曾有　亦說於因緣　譬喩幷祇夜　優波提舍經 cf. KSS 49.

other writings, though the nomenclature and the number of the items vary,[51] and it was a standard way of referring to the whole literary deposit of Buddhist tradition.[52] The point being made in the passage now considered is that the Buddha makes use of a variety of *genres* to suit a variety of dispositions. Although in principle the whole of early Buddhism has been referred to already in terms of the two or three vehicles, it is significant that the term *fang-pien* (*upāya*) is now explicitly applied to the nine-fold teaching here itemized. This brings home the fact that it is the way of understanding the whole Buddhist tradition that is at stake. In particular it should be noted that the nine-fold teaching is not rejected, any more than, as was pointed out above, *arhat*-ship is rejected. It is nevertheless seen in the new light of the dialectic of skilful means. Thus we read:

> 'I expound these nine divisions of the Dharma
> According to the capacity of sentient beings,
> As a basis to lead them into the great vehicle;
> And that is the reason for expounding this sutra.'[53]

The present sutra is not in itself offering a new teaching, but it points out the real meaning or intention of the existing teaching in nine divisions. This represents an explicit broadening out of the way in which various aspects of Buddhist teaching are referred to as skilful means.

The same tendency can be observed at the end of this first section when the buddhas are said to use their skilful means to expound the Dharma and to convert innumerable living beings so that they enter the Buddha-way,[54] and then, synonymously, the beings are said to have attained the Buddha-way if

> '. . . having heard the Dharma, they have given donations,
> Or observed the precepts and been persevering,
> If they have practiced assiduity, meditation and insight . . .'[55]

These activities (the 'six perfections') are not here explicitly identified with skilful means, but the implication is certainly that they too play an analogous intermediate role between the condition of the living beings and the state of Buddhahood.

---

[51] Conze is wrong to restrict the ninefold formula to Theravadins and Mahāsanghikas, *Thirty Years of Buddhist Studies*, p. 7, note 1.

[52] Cf. also in a later context the phrase 無數諸法門 T IX 9b, cf. KSS 59: 'countless schools of doctrine', equated with the one vehicle, though admittedly referring to the teaching of future buddhas.

[53] T IX 8a 我此九部法   隨順衆生說   入大乘爲本   以故說是經 cf. KSS 50.

[54] T IX 8c, cf. KSS 55.

[55] T IX 8c 若聞法布施   或持戒忍辱   精進禪智等 cf. KSS 55.

The longer exposition in verse (ii)

This same line of thought is now developed in detail in the second section (verses 77-95), which indeed is solely devoted to the enumeration of a great variety of practices, each of which is identified with the attainment of the Buddha-way. The only difference is that in this section it is not the central teachings or the central practices of early Buddhism but a wide proliferation of simple devotional actions such as drawing or painting images of the Buddha or paying homage at stupas or shrines with 'flowers, incense, flags and umbrellas' or even employing others to perform music.[56] Indeed the stress is on the slightness of the action, such as singing the merits of the buddhas even with a low voice, paying homage to the painted images even with distracted mind and a single flower, or entering a temple with a distracted mind and calling but once on the name of the Buddha. By all of these, and more, one is able to attain the Buddha-way. The practices are extremely simple, but the perspective is long, as is apparent from the following quotation:

> 'Even boys, in their play,
> Who, either with reed, wood or pen,
> Or with the finger-nail,
> Have drawn buddha images,
> All such ones as these,
> Gradually accumulating merit,
> And perfecting hearts of great compassion,
> Have all attained the Buddha-way;
> If they only conjure up the figures of bodhisattvas
> They bring across countless creatures.'[57]

At the time the practice may seem slight and careless, but in retrospect the intentionality of it tending towards the Buddha-way is what is reckoned to count. Everything depends on the way the act is taken. Positively taken the most minor act can have a karmic effect which ultimately links up with the far-reaching merit of the great bodhisattvas, sweeping along countless living beings to emancipation. There is another fine statement of the same idea in this same section:

> 'Or those who have offered worship,
> Were it merely by folding the hands,
> Or even raising a hand,
> Or by slightly bending the head,
> By thus paying homage to the images,
> Gradually see innumerable buddhas,

[56] T IX 9a, cf. KSS 57.

[57] T IX 9a 乃至童子戲　若草木及筆　或以指爪甲　而畫作佛像　如是諸人等　漸漸積功德　具足大悲心　皆已成佛道　但化諸菩薩　度脫無量衆 cf. KSS 57. The last two lines seem to be curious in KSS, so, with some hesitation, the interpretation of Sakamoto is followed here, *op. cit.* Vol. I p. 116.

Themselves attain the supreme way,
Extensively bring across countless creatures,
And enter nirvana without residue,
As when firewood is finished the fire dies out.'[58]

The Lotus Sutra teaches that the notion of nirvanā and the whole nine-fold teaching of the Buddha is not to be considered as other than a means or more than a means, while at the same time it teaches that actions such as slightly bending the head are also to be understood in terms of the same dialectic. In any such case there is a tussle of meanings and it is a question of not getting stuck in a provisional meaning but of resolving the tension in the right direction. Thus this section of Chapter Two represents a dramatic extension of the implications of the concept of skilful means.

Many of the practices referred to here are carried on also in non-Mahayana Buddhism, but the karmic connections are there taken in a somewhat more pedestrian way. On the one hand the promise of the simple action is not drawn out so dramatically, and on the other hand the more austere and ambitious aspects of Buddhist teaching are not criticised in the Mahayana fashion. The somewhat hierarchically ordered arrangement of the items of the Buddhist religion tends to be maintained in the Theravada form while it was laid low by the Mahayana. Nevertheless the continuities which exist in this area of popular devotion are difficult to evaluate and may be more significant than is at first sight apparent (cf. Chapter Seven on the general relevance of the concept *upāya* to Buddhism as a whole).

The longer-exposition in verse (iii)

The third section of the longer exposition in verse contains a restatement of the traditional legend about the decision of the Buddha to preach to his fellow-men after he had attained enlightenment. This narrative sequence and its relation to the pre-Mahayana account of the same decision will be considered again in a later context, as it is one of the areas in which it is possible to see the explicit dialectics of the Mahayana cradled in the thought of early Buddhism. Briefly stated however, the narrative here explains that while the Buddha was at first reluctant to teach at all because of the profundity of his experience he was strongly entreated to do so by celestial beings. Upon this he agreed to do so, using his skilful means to frame the teaching in accordance with the condition of his hearers:

'Then on remembering what former buddhas
Performed by their power of skilful means,
I resolved that the way which I had now achieved
Should be taught as three vehicles.'[59]

[58] T IX 9a 或有人禮拜　或復但合掌　乃至擧一手　或復小低頭　以此供養像　漸見無量佛　自成無上道　廣度無數衆　入無餘涅槃　如薪盡火滅 cf. KSS 58.
[59] T IX 9c 尋念過去佛　所行方便力　我今所得道　亦應說三乘 cf. KSS 63.

After teaching in terms of various distinctions he finally judged it time to 'honestly discard skilful means and only proclaim the supreme way'.[60] And as if to emphasize the appropriateness of this shift, a verse shortly following says:

> 'In the same style in which the Dharma is preached
> By the buddhas of the three worlds,
> So also do I now
> Proclaim the undivided Dharma.'[61]

This stanza fascinatingly couples the plurality of the buddhas, already stressed above in connection with the first chapter of the sutra, with the not-divided-Dharma. It also emphasizes the *manner* of the activity of a buddha, the term for style[62] suggesting a formalisation, almost a ritualisation, of this activity.

The idea of a progression within the Buddha's teaching is the seed for the later *p'an-chiao* systems developed in China, and adumbrated also in the *Wu Liang I Ching* (J. *Muryōgikyō*),[63] the sutra which commonly is used as a preface to The Lotus Sutra itself in the T'ien T'ai and dependent traditions. This development need not be considered here in detail but it is worth noting that the idea of two stages in the teaching, which later became several stages, is closely connected with the manner or style of the teaching. This style, based on skilful means, involves setting up a teaching based on discrimination and then resolving it in favour of the undivided teaching.

The term skilful means is related to both of these steps. It is sometimes felt that the theory of progression in the teaching of the Buddha is merely a justification for a new teaching which is being put into his mouth. Yet this would be a crude interpretation. The 'new' teaching does not have any 'content' in the sense in which this would be necessary for the charge to stick. The new teaching is rather about the style, direction and meaning of the existing teaching. The term skilful means explains the relationship between the initial setting up of the teaching and its resolution into the ultimate meaning of Buddhism. These two steps are two aspects of one movement of spiritual experience They belong together, except that from the point of view of those being taught by the Buddha there seems to be a progression from one to the other. This progression is not only developed in the later *p'an-chiao* systems, but also comes out in The Lotus Sutra itself in the recognition by Śāriputra of his own development (in Chapter III of the

---

[60] T IX 10a 正直捨方便　但說無上道 cf. KSS 65.

[61] T IX 10a 如三世諸佛　說法之儀式　我今亦如是　說無分別法 cf. KSS 65. 'Past, present and future' in the latter is an explanatory gloss.

[62] 儀式 (see previous note).

[63] 無量義經 A first English translation prepared by various hands was published by the Risshō Kōsei-kai, Tokyo 1974 under the title: *Muryōgikyō, The Sutra of Innumerable Meanings and Kanfugen-gyō, The Sutra of Meditation on the Bodhisattva Universal Virtue.* It is thought that the sutra may have been composed in China. See also below, chapter Four, note 22.

Sutra) and in the parable of the returning son (see below, Chapter Three). In the present passage the main emphasis is of course on the Buddha's own recognition of what is appropriate to the developing situation. At the same time this itself implies that each step is in accordance with the readiness of his hearers. At first the stress is on their incapacity and the consequent teaching of the triple vehicle through the power of skilful means; only then they are considered ready to advance to the 'undivided Dharma'. The activity of the Buddha himself is consistent in its intention, and the progression merely reflects the way it must appear in the narrative form. Yet the two steps of the teaching represent a real enough progression on the part of the hearers, for they must move from an acceptance of the Buddha's teaching on the basis of ignorance to a rejection of it on the basis of enlightenment. The term *fang-pien*, skilful means, is the notion which demands this achievement, and thus without adding anything particularly 'new' in the sense of content it indicates what the existing teaching is really for.

The terminological details of the whole section reaffirm the main themes of previous parts of the chapter. The buddhas have 'faultless insight'[64] not only into the way things really are,[65] which they come to know on the 'throne of enlightenment'[66] but also specifically into the character of all living beings. They know their 'conduct . . . what they entertain in their deepest minds, the karma they have developed in the past, their inclinations and zeal, and their capacities, keen or dull'.[67] On the one hand the wisdom which the Buddha has attained is 'wonderful and supreme'[68] while on the other hand 'all beings are dull in their capacities, attached to pleasure and blind with ignorance'.[69] Various terms for the unified meaning of diverse teachings in this context are 'the one vehicle',[70] 'the Buddha-vehicle',[71] 'the one-vehicle way'[72] 'this most

[64] T IX 9b 無漏智, cf. KSS 59.

[65] T IX 9b 知法常無性 'knowing dharmas to be permanently without specific nature', cf. KSS 59. The whole context here has been variously interpreted, see Sakamoto's notes, *op. cit.* Vol. I p. 354. It seems unlikely that the clause just below should be translated 'the word abides for ever' if it means that it is always to be conceived of as subject to karma (cf. Sakamoto). The permanence lies in Karma being fundamentally vacuous (縁起の法は自体が空であるから Sakamoto, p.353). Cf. also explanatory footnotes in KSS, p. 60. This passage is a good example of the danger of a translation drifting into a metaphysics which was never really intended (contrast the leaving aside of 'whether things are or whether they are not', 若有若無, cf. note 44 above). One might tentatively suggest for 世間相常住 in its context: 'the character of the world is always thus'. Iwamoto, *op. cit.* Vol. I p. 121, takes the passage to be about the unchanging character of the Dharma as teaching in the world, and not to be about dharmas as factors of existence at all.

[66] T IX 9b 於道場知已 Cf. KSS 60. 道場 is a standard term for which KSS has 'Wisdom-throne'.

[67] T IX 9b 知衆生諸行　深心之所念　過去所習業　欲性精進力　及諸根利鈍　cf. KSS 61.

[68] T IX 9c 我所得智慧　微妙最第一 cf. KSS 62.

[69] T IX 9c 衆生諸根鈍　著樂癡所盲 cf. KSS 62.

[70] T IX 9b 一乘.

[71] T IX 9b 佛乘.

[72] T IX 10b 一乘道.

wonderful supreme Dharma',[73] 'the unsurpassed way'[74] and 'the supreme Nirvana'.[75] These are all more or less synonymous and stand in a dialectical relationship to the divided or discriminated teaching.

The term nirvana needs special consideration because it is used, so to speak, on both sides of the fence. The 'supreme Nirvana' mentioned above has as its shadow the 'voice of nirvana' or more literally the 'sound of nirvana' heard at the very first preaching of the Buddha along with the teaching distinguishing *arhats*, the Dharma and the *sangha*.[76] All of these are on the provisional side. The 'Dharma of nirvana' is the constant teaching of the Buddha, in so far as he is teaching in a manner designed to end distress.[77] Strictly speaking the 'nirvana nature of all dharmas' is inexpressible, and it is only taught by the Buddha's power of skilful means.[78] Two different terms seem to distinguish subtly *Nirvana* as a cypher for the inexpressible, valuable meaning, and *nirvana* as that provisionally taught for the ending of ill.[79] Recognising the 'nirvana-nature of all dharmas' ultimately subverts the necessity for teaching nirvana as an end to distress and suffering, but the latter was first necessary and continues to be so for the benefit of living beings still 'sunk in suffering'.[80] It must be admitted that the reference to the possibility of the Buddha himself 'entering' nirvana instead of preaching makes use of the term for the discriminated nirvana,[81]—but then it is precisely such a nirvana which the Buddha transcends when he decides to preach! Because of the incapacity of beings he can only preach that which he himself has just had to refuse. Yet by so preaching on the discriminated side he can eventually bring others to the pure, balanced Buddahood which carries the same rejection of the discriminated nirvana and the same compassion for beings still 'sunk in suffering'.

Another prominent feature of this section is the assertion of the universal intention of the teaching. This is formulated in the 'original vow' of the buddhas.[82] The vow runs:

> 'As to the Buddha-way which I tread,
> I desire universally to cause all living beings
> To attain the same way along with me.'[83]

[73] T IX 9c最妙第一法. Also described as 'the mystery of all the buddhas': ... 是妙法諸佛之祕... T IX 10b, cf. KSS 66-7.

[74] T IX 10a 無上道.

[75] T IX 9b 第一寂滅.

[76] T IX 10a 是名轉法輪　便有涅槃音　及以阿羅漢　法僧差別名 cf. KSS 64.

[77] T IX 10a 讚示涅槃法　生死苦永盡 cf. KSS 64.

[78] T IX 10c 諸法寂滅相　不可以言宣　以方便力故　爲五比丘說 cf. KSS 64.

[79] 涅槃 for the discriminated teaching, and 寂滅 for final nirvana, or original nirvana. Cf. also the quotations in notes 46 and 47 above, and contrast 涅槃 with 眞滅.

[80] T IX 9c 衆生沒在苦 cf. KSS 62.

[81] T IX 9c 我寧不說法　疾入於涅槃 cf. KSS 63.

[82] T IX 9b 諸佛本誓願 This is a common feature of Mahāyāna Buddhism of course, for every bodhisattva makes a great vow to serve all beings. It comes to greatest prominence in the Pure Land Buddhist tradition based on the 'original vow' (J. *hongan* 本願) of Amitābha Buddha and the temples named after this vow in Japan (J. *Honganji*).

[83] T IX 9b 我所行佛道　普欲令衆生　亦同得此道 cf. KSS 59.

The phrase 'all living beings' recurs constantly,[84] and the universalism is reinforced by the buddhas themselves being as numerous as the sands of the Ganges.[85] There are no doubt some beings who will scorn the teaching, and discernment is necessary to be able to benefit from it even though it is taught by skilful means.[86] But those who hear it need have no further doubts, since they know that the buddhas teach through skilful means and that they themselves will become buddhas.[87]

The role of the term *fang-pien* in this second chapter of Kumārajīva's translation of the Lotus Sutra is in its outlines a consistent one. Almost anything in the whole range of Buddhist teaching and practice can be described as *fang-pien* or skilful means. This applies not only to a Buddha-image playfully drawn with the finger-nail but also to such a central teaching as that of nirvana itself. If a narrative account is given of the intentions and actions of a Buddha, then *fang-pien* means that provisional teachings are established only to be dissolved in favour of 'the most wonderful supreme Dharma'. For this latter numerous synonyms are available, but it appears to be impossible to say anything directly about it. Only those things which work as *fang-pien* offer a way to indicate it, and in so far as they work, they bring about their own redundancy. If one turns attention to the development of the living beings under tutelage, the dialectic of *fang-pien* remains the same. The benefit which they reap from the discriminated teachings enables them to move forward to the undiscriminated. This move also involves perplexity and doubt, giving way to recognition and joy. The teaching about *fang-pien* offers no new 'content' in any ordinary sense. Rather it is about the nature, purpose, direction or style of Buddhist teaching and practice. It characterises the operation of the Buddhist religion.

---

[84] Preferable to 'creatures', to avoid misunderstanding. No doctrine of their creation is intended.

[85] T IX 9b 現在十方佛　其數如恒沙 cf. KSS 60.

[86] T IX 10b 當來世惡人　聞佛說一乘　迷惑不信受　破法墮惡道...以萬億方便　隨宜而說法　其不習學者　不能曉了此cf. KSS 67.

[87] T IX 10b 汝等既已知　諸佛世之師　隨宜方便事　無復諸疑惑　心生大歡喜　自知當作佛 cf. KSS 67.

3 STORIES ABOUT SKILFUL MEANS IN THE LOTUS SUTRA

The burning house

There are several allegorical stories in the Lotus Sutra which illustrate in various ways the principle of skilful means. Sometimes these are taken merely as attempts to justify the apparent emergence of the Mahayana as a schismatic school within Buddhism. Although there undoubtedly is an element of this, the main point of them seems to be rather the relationship between the articulated forms of Buddhist teaching, which are varied, and the ultimate intention of it, which lies beyond or behind those forms. The stories are not very systematically arranged and they may have been composed at various stages in the compilation of the sutra. For Sino-Japanese Buddhism however they are all of more or less equal status and for present purposes they may be treated together. The stories have been widely known in East Asia, partly no doubt because stories are easier to remember than philosophical dialogues, but partly also because they have often formed the subject of paintings.

One of the most widely known is certainly that of the burning house. It appears in the third chapter of the sutra, following on from the chapter on skilful means which it is intended to illustrate. Of all the chapters in The Lotus Sutra this one contains the second largest number of occurrences of the term skilful means (see Appendix C).

Since translations of the story of the burning house have now found their way into popular anthologies, and since it is rather verbose when given in full, a very brief summary of the story itself will suffice here. A wealthy old man has a great house with only one door. The house is in a decrepit state, and a fire breaks out, threatening to engulf all the man's children who are absorbed in play within the house. The old man calls them in vain, then resorts in desperation to skilful means (*fang-pien*). Knowing the kinds of things which they all like he calls out that there are goat-carts, deer-carts and bullock-carts waiting for them outside the door. Upon this they all come scrambling out of the house and are saved from the flames. The three kinds of carts are nowhere to be seen, but instead the old man gives to each one a still more splendid chariot, beautifully ornate and drawn by a white bullock.

The question is then raised, by way of comment on the story, as to whether the old man was guilty of a falsehood. Śāriputra's answer to this is that he was not, but it is not only this judgement which is interesting but also its justification. The emphasis is put not on the fact that the children received a better vehicle than intended, which might after all be taken to cover their failure to receive the specific kinds which were originally promised. Rather, the discrepancy is justified by the fulfilment of the old man's intention to bring them out from the flames. Even if they had not received any cart at all it would have been inappropriate to speak of a falsehood, because the original thought of the old man was: 'I will get my children to escape by a skilful means.'[1]

Given the above fundamental line of interpretation, the giving of superior chariots equally to all does not appear inconsistent either. On the contrary, it is important because it subverts the distinction between the various kinds of vehicle enumerated in the first instance in order to get the children out of the fire. These were referred to in variety to begin with because the old man knew 'that to which each of the children is predisposed, and all the various attractive playthings and curiosities to which their natures will joyfully respond'.[2] When they all receive the same superior chariot in the end, this underlines the overriding consistency of the old man's action by contrast with the various inconsistent and ultimately irrelevant interests of the children.

After Śāriputra's initial answer that the old man is not guilty of falsehood there follows a longer allegorical explanation of the story. According to this the old man is the Tathāgata (the Buddha), the house is the world, and the children are the inhabitants of the world. These inhabitants are too blinded by their sufferings, and by their foolish attachments, to be able to be saved from the round of birth and death by a direct exposure to the spiritual power and wisdom of the Tathāgata. Hence he makes use of the three vehicles, namely the *śrāvaka-yāna*, the *pratyekabuddha-yāna* and the *buddha-yāna*, as a skilful means.[3] These three vehicles are identified with the goat-cart, the deer-cart and the bullock-cart respectively and the basic implication is that various paths within Buddhism are distinguished because of varying needs while all of them have the same fundamental intention and meaning.

There is a complication at this point because the third vehicle is referred to again as 'the great vehicle' (i.e. the mahāyāna), while one who follows it is a bodhisattva or a *mahāsattva*, that is an 'enlightenment-being' or a 'great being'.[4] At the same time the vehicle which all receive equally at the end is *also* called the *mahāyāna*.[5] This may seem, at first sight, to be polemics in favour of the third vehicle of the three, namely that of the bodhisattvas or

---

[1] T IX 13a（是長者先作是意）我以方便令子得出 cf. KSS 86. This picks up the story itself: T IX 12c 我今當設方便令諸子等得免斯害。, 'Let me now set up some skilful means to get my children to escape this disaster', cf. KSS 84.

[2] T IX 12c 父知諸子先心各有所好。種種珍玩奇異之物情必樂著。cf. KSS 84.

[3] T IX 13b 當得三乘聲聞辟支佛佛乘。cf. KSS 88. N.B. buddha-vehicle, rather than bodhisattva-vehicle, but see below.

[4] T IX 13b, cf. KSS 89. Mahāyāna is always translated into Chinese as 大乘 (literally great vehicle'), while *mahāsattva* is transcribed (as is *bodhisattva*); thus there is a loss of the word-association between *mahāyāna* and *mahāsattva*.

[5] T IX 13c 然後但以大乘而度脫之。cf. KSS 90. The Sanskrit term is used in discussion for familiarity's sake, though it is translated (literally) into Chinese, and not transliterated. It is italicized to indicate that reference is being made to the text rather than to Mahayana Buddhism generally.

mahāsattvas as opposed to those of the *śrāvakas* and *pratyekabuddhas*. However, such an interpretation would fail to take into account that the third vehicle, as a differentiated vehicle, is itself superseded in so far as all three are replaced by the single consistent vehicle. Any polemical interpretation would depend on a continued differentiation between the three. The real intention, despite the equivocal use of the term *mahāyāna*, seems to be to maintain a consistent interpretation which goes beyond polemics, and indeed this is brought out by the concluding comments in the text. Thus: 'There is no falsehood in first preaching three vehicles to attract all living creatures, and afterwards saving by the great vehicle only.'[6] It is only because of the inability of the beings to receive the Mahayana teaching[7] directly that 'the buddhas, on account of their power of skilful means, in the one buddha-vehicle distinguish and expound the three.'[8]

The term 'buddha-vehicle' is used equivocally just as is *mahāyāna*. Sometimes it refers to the third of the three, as earlier,[9] but sometimes, as in the case quoted immediately above, it is not a further differentiated vehicle, neither a third nor a fourth. Rather it refers, in this special sense, to that single vehicle which takes over when the differentiated vehicles are seen in their true character as skilful means. This one buddha-vehicle, according to the parallel section in verse, brings bodhisattvas and *śrāvakas* alike directly to the 'throne of enlightenment'.[10] Thus the buddha-vehicle which transcends the differentiated vehicles is also radically identified with them. As the verse goes on to say: 'Apart from the skilful means of the Buddha, there is no other vehicle to be found.'[11]

This allegory confirms the pattern of thinking already observed in Chapter II of the sutra, and indeed the text introduces it as doing exactly that. 'Did I not say before that the buddhas, the world-honoured ones, proclaim the Dharma by various karmic reasonings, parables, forms of words and skilful means, all for the sake of supreme, perfect enlightenment?'[12] The phrase listing forms of teaching occurs half a dozen times in Chapter II, as well as again here, and symbolizes articulated Buddhist tradition in general. The meditational or spiritual aspects of Buddhist religion, if these may be referred to separately from the conceptual formulations, are also treated as part of

---

[6] T IX 13c 無有虛妄。初說三乘引導眾生。然後但以大乘而度脫之。cf. KSS 90.

[7] 大乘法, Mahayana-Dharma.

[8] T IX 13c 諸佛方便力故於一佛乘分別說三。cf. KSS 90.

[9] See quotation in note 3 above.

[10] T IX 15a 與諸菩薩　及聲聞眾　乘此寶乘　直至道場 cf. KSS 103.

[11] T IX 15a 更無餘乘除佛方便 cf. KSS 103.

Cf. T IX 15a 諸佛世尊　雖以方便　所化眾生　皆是菩薩 'Although the buddhas, the world-honoured ones, use skilful means, the living beings whom they convert are all bodhisattvas', cf. KSS 104.

[12] T IX 12b 我先不言諸佛世尊以種種因緣譬喻言辭方便說法。皆爲阿耨多羅三藐三菩提耶。cf. KSS 82. 'Supreme perfect enlightenment' is given in transliterated form for *anuttara samyak sambodhi*, and should perhaps strictly be so rendered to convey what Kumārajīva's readers had before them.

the whole matter to be understood in terms of skilful means. In the interpretation of the story we read as follows: 'By these skilful means the
Tathāgata entices living beings and says to them: "You should know that
these three vehicles have all been praised by sages. You will be free in
yourselves and not seek to rely on anything else. Riding these three vehicles
you will use the perfect faculties and powers, the perceptions, the way, the
concentrations, emancipations and contemplations, you will be happy in
yourselves and gain infinite peace and joy".'[13] Therefore, all in all, it is the
Buddhist religion as a whole which is to be understood as arising from the
Buddha's use of skilful means.

In the verses the four noble truths are also brought into this context. The
term skilful means is just slipped in with the second truth:

> 'If there are any living beings
> Who do not know the origin of suffering,
> And are deeply attached to the cause of suffering,
> And cannot for one moment abandon it;
> For all their sakes
> I preach the way as skilful means,
> Saying that the cause of all suffering
> Lies in desire.'[14]

Of course if it is applied to one, the term skilful means could be applied to
any or all of the four truths. In any case it is closely linked with the preaching
of 'the way', which except when specifically defining the fourth truth, refers
to Buddhist teaching as a whole.

This understanding of the four truths is reinforced by its context in a
general argument about the teaching of nirvana.

> 'Though I previously proclaimed
> That you would cross into extinction,
> It was only the exhaustion of birth-and-death,
> And really it was not extinction.'[15]

---

[13] T IX 13b 如來以是方便誘進衆生。復作是言。汝等當知。此三乘法皆是聖所稱歎。
自在無繫無所依求。乘是三乘。以無漏根力覺道禪定解脱三昧等。而自娛樂。便得無量
安隱快樂。cf. KSS 88.

[14] T IX 15a 若有衆生　不知苦本　深著苦因　不能暫捨　爲是等故　方便說道　諸苦所
因　貪欲爲本 cf. KSS 104-5. This occurrence of *fang-pien* is not reflected by any equivalent
phrase in Dharmarakṣa's version or in the Sanskrit texts, and though Kumārajīva's text
may have been an archaic one this may be a gloss attributable to him. Verse translation is
particularly prone to minor contractions or additions, to obtain the correct number of
characters for a line, and precisely because these may not have seemed particularly important
at the time they indicate how the text was being understood by the translator as he worked.

[15] T IX 15a 我雖先說　汝等滅度　但盡生死　而實不滅 cf. KSS 103-4. Cf. also the
longer passage just after the rehearsal of the four truths in this context T IX 15b, KSS 105.
The term used for extinction here both times is the same: 滅, but it is used equivocally.

This is part of a concentration on the teaching about nirvana or extinction which becomes increasingly prominent in subsequent chapters of the sutra. The main point for the present is that the initial teaching of extinction is given because of the unenlightened beings' submersion in the sufferings of birth-and-death (equals Skt. *saṃsāra*). This contrasted differentiation between *saṃsāra* and nirvana was articulated as a skilful means, but in itself it is not 'Buddha-insight', which remains to be sought,[16] nor 'entire emancipation' nor 'the supreme way'.[17]

The son who does not recognise himself

Another well known story is that of the son who does not recognise himself, found in Chapter IV of the sutra. It is not told by the Buddha but by four senior monks, Subhūti, Kātyāyana, Kāśyapa and Maudgalyāyana, to express their recognition of the enlightenment predicted for Śāriputra and by implication for all *śrāvakas*.[18] Thus the emphasis in the story is on the recognition of the meaning by the disciples as much as on the exposition of it by the Buddha. This is recognised in Kumārajīva's title for the chapter: 'Faith and Understanding.'[19]

The story, though rather long, can be briefly summarised. A young man leaves his father and wanders abroad for years. He is reduced to utter poverty and later accidentally comes to the city where his father in the meantime has become very wealthy. The father recognises the son, but the son does not recognise the father. The father wishes to receive his son as heir to his new wealth but when he sends messengers the son is thoroughly scared by their attentions, fearing the worst. The father realises the psychological difficulty of the son and therefore changes his policy. He does not reveal his relationship to him but instead orders the messengers to set him free and arranges menial work for him to do. Gradually he gives him more responsibility and better pay, slowly building up his confidence until he can treat him as an adopted son and give him responsibility for the whole estate. At last the father, who is near the end of his life, calls together many witnesses and declares the whole story, revealing the true, original relationship.

Three actions of the father in the story are explicitly referred to as skilful means. Firstly, when he realises that the abject disposition of his son compared with his own high estate are simply too much for the son to cope with, '. . . out of skilful means he does not say to others, "This is my son" '.[20]

---

[16] T IX 15a 今所應作　唯佛智慧 cf. KSS 104.

[17] T IX 15b 一切解脱 and 無上道 respectively, cf. KSS 105.

[18] Cf. the whole introductory passage, T IX 16, KSS 116-7, and especially: 'In the Buddha's presence we now hear the prediction of *śrāvakas* to *anuttara-samyak-sambodhi*' (我等今於佛前聞授聲阿耨多羅三藐三菩提記。）

[19] 信解, translated in KSS as 'Faith-Discernment'. Sanskrit has *Adhimukti*, 'Disposition'. (The KSS note on the title of this chapter is very puzzling.)

[20] T IX 17a 以方便不語他人云是我子。cf. KSS 120.

Presumably this is because any such declaration would merely disrupt the situation which is about to be so carefully devised, just as the original attempt to have the son brought before him was counter-productive. Secondly, in order to attract his son 'he sets up a skilful means'[21] which consists in allowing him to shovel dirt away for double wages. Thirdly the father himself puts on working clothes and goes to urge on the workmen. 'By this skilful means he is able to get near to his son',[22] so that he can offer him more wages and security, praise his diligence and intimate that he is willing to adopt him. Each of these three actions is necessary because of the disposition of the son himself, each involves a provisional disguising of the true situation (for even the shovelling away of the dirt is a task invented to serve the purpose), and when all is done each of the skilful means is superseded or redundant. Indeed they have to be set quite aside for the full realisation of the purpose to be brought about. As for the son's disposition, it progresses from fear to perplexity and a degree of confidence, until finally satisfaction with what he thinks he has himself achieved through his diligent labour is replaced by joy over quite unexpected treasure.

In the interpretation given in the text itself, after the story, the rich father is identified with the Buddha while the son is taken to represent his disciples. The disciples declare themselves to be all, as it were, sons of the Buddha, and that the Tathāgata has always declared them to be his sons.[23] It was they themselves who had not recognised it, and therefore the Buddha, who knew that they took delight in lesser teachings, taught them according to their capacity by his power of skilful means.[24] Not that the Buddha himself simply acquiesces in the lesser teachings, for 'the world-honoured one by his power of skilful means expounds the insight of the *tathāgatas*.'[25] It is the disciples themselves who can only partially understand and who therefore need formulations which provide a provisional satisfaction.

To some extent a polemical element is also involved, in so far as the disciples are made to admit that they were previously satisfied with inferior or lesser teaching,[26] which is treated as equivalent to the dirt which the poor son was happy to shovel away. At the same time the polemical element is recognised and superseded in the text itself, which goes on: 'In this sutra he now proclaims one vehicle only; and though formerly in front of the bodhisattvas he spoke disparagingly of the *śrāvakas* who were pleased with lesser

[21] T IX 17a 設方便 cf. KSS 120. This is another example of the conscious devising and establishment (設) of skilful means.

[22] T IX 17a 以方便故得近其子, cf. KSS 121.

[23] T IX 17b 我等皆似佛子 and 如來常說我等爲子, cf. KSS 123. Note that this is quite clearly understood as a simile arising out of the story, and is not an indication of incipient theism.

[24] T IX 17c 佛知我等心樂小法。以方便力隨我等說。cf. KSS 124.

[25] T IX 17b 世尊以方便力說如來智慧 cf. KSS 123.

[26] T IX 17b 小法 (twice), cf. KSS 123. Cf. the term 小乘, *hīnayāna*, which could not be far from the minds of Kumārajīva's readers.

teaching, yet in reality he was converting them with the teaching of the *mahāyāna*.'[27] According to this standpoint, the Mahayana does not seek an exclusive differentiation of vehicles, some to be confirmed and some to be rejected, but rather it implies an inclusive universalism. Even though some sentences seem to give special eminence to the bodhisattva vehicle, the final words of this chapter (in the verse sequence) present the buddhas' activity as follows:

> 'According to how all the living beings
> In previous lives put down good roots,
> They have knowledge of the mature
> And of those who are immature,
> They take it all into account,
> Articulate it in their understanding,
> And following the way of the one vehicle
> They appropriately expound the three.'[28]

Leaving aside the polemical entanglements, and their resolution, the story clearly conveys also, just like that of the burning house, a general understanding of the nature of religious teaching in Buddhism. It picturesquely illustrates how certain elements in the teaching as a whole are less than ultimately true. However they are supposed not to be fraudulent, because they are psychologically necessary in the initial stages. Without a certain amount of dissimulatory packaging it would not be possible to convey the essence at all. One may surmise that if the ultimate contents of the packaging turned out to be disappointing or less valuable than the package itself then objections would be in order. The charge would be deceit. However the result given in the story is not a charge of deceit but an expression of surprise and gratitude and joy. The final decision or response in this connection is not a matter for the observer to judge as observer. What must be noted is that various aspects of graded Buddhist guidance are clearly thought of as provisional, and that they find their ultimate resolution and dismissal in the successful appropriation of the Buddhist meaning.

The rain-cloud and other similes

The leading parable of Chapter V is about a large rain-cloud which waters a variety of plants, and it is the plants or 'herbs' which have provided the chapter with its title: 'The Parable of the Herbs'.[29] Although the variety of

[27] T IX 17c 於此經中唯說一乘。而昔於菩薩前毀呰聲聞樂小法者。然佛實以大乘教化。cf. KSS 124.

[28] T IX 19a 隨諸衆生　宿世善根　又知成熟　未成熟者　種種籌量　分別知已　於一乘道　隨宜說三。cf. KSS 137.

[29] T IX 19a, 藥草喩, cf. KSS 139. The medicinal character of some plants has nothing whatever to do with the argument of this chapter, and seems to be an accidental association. Herbs, that is, medicinal plants, simply feature among other plants in a list of those watered by the rain.

the plants and the amount of moisture they need is part of the point of the parable, the consistency of the rain is if anything more important, and it may be that the parable was originally expanded on the basis of a widely used simile found in Chapter I of The Lotus Sutra itself. One of the closing verses there reads:

'The Buddha will pour the rain of Dharma
To satisfy those who seek the way.'[30]

This chapter again contains some reference to the relationship between *śrāvakas* and bodhisattvas, but the main emphasis is on a much more general statement of the nature of the Buddha's teaching. The opening passage states this quite clearly:

'The Tathāgata is the king of all teachings and all the things which he declares are free from falsehood. He uses his insight-led skilful means with respect to all teachings and so expounds them. These teachings which he proclaims lead right into the stage of all-knowledge. The Tathāgata sees and knows all teachings and their final meaning, and he also knows what all living beings are doing in their inmost hearts. He penetrates these matters without hindrance, and having a profound understanding of all teachings he manifests perfect insight to all living beings.'[31] There is some equivocation in the original with respect to the term here translated as teachings, and it should perhaps more literally be rendered 'law' or 'laws'. Yet this would have little meaning in English. The same term, representing Sanskrit 'Dharma', or 'dharmas', can be used both for the normative teaching of the Buddha, his 'Law' or Dharma, and in the plural for the factors of existence into which the world of our experience is analysed in Buddhist thought. Though we might expect 'King of Dharma' (cf. Skt. *dharmarāja*) we definitely find in Kumāra-jīva's version 'king of dharmas', which Sakamoto takes to be 'teachings' in the plural.[32] This is moreover actually in agreement with the Sanskrit.[33] Sakamoto also takes that which the Buddha expounds by his skilful means referred to in the subsequent sentence to be various kinds of teaching such as moral teachings, the four noble truths, the teaching of dependent origination, and the six perfections.[34] In a sense the analysis of existence into its constituent factors is indeed included in such teachings, and it is in this full sense that the term 'teachings' is to be taken above. It includes all the denotable

[30] T IX 5b 佛當雨法雨充足求道者 cf. KSS 31. Cf. also J. J. Jones, *The Mahāvastu*, Vol. I, p. 211.

[31] T IX 19a 如來是諸法之王若有所說皆不虛也。於一切法以智方便而演說之。其所說法。皆悉到於一切智地。如來觀知一切諸法之所歸趣。亦知一切衆生深心所行。通達無礙。又於諸法究盡明了。示諸衆生一切智慧。cf. KSS 139.

[32] Sakamoto, *op. cit.* p. 264, and note *ad loc.* takes it to be 'teachings' in the plural, もろもろの法（教）. It seems necessary to keep the plural for the subsequent cases of 法 and some equivocation between dharmas as teachings and as factors of existence seems unavoidable and not necessarily undesirable in a passage such as this.

[33] Wogihara and Tsuchida, *op. cit.* p. 114 line 7: *sarva-dharmāṇāṃ rājā* . . .

[34] Sakamoto, *op. cit.* note *ad loc.*

factors which the Buddha in his insight and skilful means points out. The
Buddha has a freely discursive grasp of these which enables him to correlate
the intention or final meaning[35] of given factors or teachings with the inmost
dispositions of the living beings whom he teaches. There is no fraud, it is
argued, in the sense that the discriminated teachings find their fulfilment, or
their resolution, in perfect insight itself.

The parable is not really a story so much as an extended simile. A single
great cloud pours down rain all over the world, giving moisture equally to
plants, trees, thickets and forests of all sizes. Each organism develops in its
own way, blossoms and bears its fruit, 'yet although the same soil makes
them grow and the same rain waters them the plants and trees are all
different.'[36] The explanation, if not already obvious, is given in the text itself
along the following lines. The Tathāgata is like the cloud and the great sound
of his voice goes out over the whole world just as the rain-cloud does. He
knows the dispositions and abilities of all the beings in the world, and proclaims the same Dharma to them all in various ways so that they can benefit
from it. Only the Tathāgata can clearly perceive the stages in which living
beings find themselves. They themselves do not understand this clearly, just
as the plants and trees have no knowledge of their relative size. Nor can living
beings immediately or directly accept the undivided Dharma, because they
are hindered by the great variety of thoughts which they entertain. Hence
the teaching is related to these thoughts and to the practices which seem so
indispensable to them. In reality however the Dharma is as unified as the
rain-cloud. What then is the purport of this undivided Dharma, or to what
does it tend? The answer is given in a couple of parallel formulations of which
the first runs: 'The Dharma proclaimed by the Tathāgata is of one character
and of one flavour, that is to say, it is marked with deliverance, non-
attachment, extinction, and finally brings one to comprehensive knowledge.'[37]
Extinction here does not mean annihilation but rather that nirvana of a
Tathāgata with respect to which the dichotomy of annihilation or existence
is no longer applicable. The second formulation is: 'The Tathāgata knows
this Dharma of one character and one flavour, marked, that is to say, with
deliverance, non-attachment and extinction, marked with ultimate nirvana
and permanently restful extinction, ending in return to empty space.'[38]

The term skilful means does not occur explicitly in the prose form of the
simile nor in the appended explanation, though it does appear in the intro-

---

[35] 歸趣. Cf. sentence quoted earlier: 'We too on receiving this Dharma can attain Nirvana.
But now we do not know to what this principle tends.' (T IX 6b 我等亦得此法到於涅槃。
而今不知是義所趣。)

[36] T IX 19b 雖一地所生一雨所潤而諸草木各有差別。cf. KSS 140.

[37] T IX 19b 如來說法一相一味。所謂解脫相離滅相。究竟至於一切種智。cf. KSS 142.

[38] T IX 19c 如來知是一相一味之法。所謂解脫相離相滅相。究竟涅槃常寂滅相。終
歸於空。cf. KSS 143. 'Nirvana' and 'extinction' are more or less synonymous here. This
simile is not concerned with the status of the initial teaching of nirvana. 'The void' is eschewed
here because it is so often a mistranslation for *śūnyatā*. 空 is regularly used for *śūnyā* or
śūnyatā, but in fact Wogihara and Tsuchida, *op. cit.* p. 116, have *ākāśa* in this case.

ductory passage as quoted already above. It also appears twice in the verse form of the simile in direct explanation of its meaning.

'The Buddha's equal teaching
Is like one sort of rain,
But according to the nature of living beings
What they receive is not the same,
Just as these plants and trees
Each take a varying supply.
In accordance with this parable
The Buddha makes things known through skilful means
And with varying terminology
He proclaims the one Dharma;
While out of the Buddha's own insight
It is like one drop in the sea.'[39]

The verse form of the simile also allegorises the different types of plants, making various kinds of disciples and *pratyekabuddhas* the smaller and larger herbs respectively, bodhisattvas the shrubs and especially advanced and effective bodhisattvas the trees. The polemical aspect is however of slight importance in this passage, and additional material in the Sanskrit text tradition plays it down still further. Admittedly the closing lines of Kumārajīva's verse say that the *śrāvakas* do not attain extinction, while those directly addressed are told that they will pursue the bodhisattva way until they become buddhas. On the other hand the unity and equality of the Buddha's teaching has already been thoroughly avowed by the whole chapter, and it seems consistent to say that the *śrāvakas* will not attain the final goal in their capacity as *śrāvakas*. Even the bodhisattvas are only predicted to buddhahood in this context after gradual discipline, and they are not equated with the buddhas over against the disciples.[40]

Extensions of this chapter which are not found in Kumārajīva's version contain two further similes. One speaks of a series of pots made out of the same clay by the same potter, but used for storing different things such as sugar, ghee, curds and milk. The meaning is the same as that of the rain and the plants. The second is a longer story about a blind man who recovers his sight as a result of healing, and who thereupon thinks of his power to see as an unsurpassed achievement, only to be told that there is much else which he could still attain such as supernormal powers. It is of some interest that the four herbs used to cure his blindness are allegorised as 'voidness, signlessness, wishlessness and attaining nirvana',[41] so that in effect all of these must be

---

[39] T IX 20b 佛平等說　如一味雨　隨眾生性　所受不同　如彼草木　所稟各異　佛
以此喻　方便開示　種種言辭　演說一法　於佛智慧　如海一渧 KSS 149. Cf. also a standard formula near the end of the verse, T IX 20b and KSS 151.

[40] T IX 20b 汝等所行　是菩薩道　漸漸修學　悉當成佛 cf. KSS 151.

[41] Wogihara and Tsuchida, *op. cit.* p. 126: *śunyatā' nimittāpraṇihita-nirvāṇa-dvāraṃ*. The passage not contained in Kumārajīva's version runs from the end of the first long verse section, and may be consulted (with caution) in Kern, *op. cit.* pp. 128-141.

supposed to be on the level of skilful means. The three vehicles are in this passage too said to be shown by the skilfulness in means of the Tathāgata,[42] and no matter what one's disposition or one's route there will only be one nirvana, and not two or three as Kāśyapa was wondering.[43] In general these extra passages do not seem to add anything of fundamental importance to the general position of the sutra, and since Kumārajīva did not include them they will not be considered any further here.

Stories of unexpected treasure

The jewel is a regular image in Buddhism. The story of the son who did not recognise himself, discussed earlier, and told by the four head monks to express recognition of their newly found treasure, is prefaced by a simile of a jewel. They congratulate themselves on 'obtaining an incalculably rare jewel without themselves seeking it'.[44] The same simile of a jewel is used as the basis for two further stories in Chapter VIII and Chapter XIV.

The second of these, in Chapter XIV, is itself really little more than an extended simile. It tells of a powerful king who wins great victories and rewards his military men lavishly, according to their merit. All kinds of treasures are handed out, but only the jewel worn on his own head is kept back, as it would be astonishing indeed if he were to give away his own special emblem. At the very last, when his army is doing battle as never before, he does indeed disburse it as a present to them all. The interpretation is woven into the story itself and explains how the teaching of nirvana is among the preliminary rewards, while the final reward symbolised by the jewel on the king's own head is nothing less than The Lotus Sutra.

There is no mention of skilful means throughout the prose version of the story, but there are two occurrences in the verse account (and two other general occurrences in the chapter as a whole). As might be expected, the preliminary rewards are described as skilful means. This follows what is by now an accustomed pattern, except for the introduction of *sutras* into the picture as well as *dharmas*, to indicate the Buddha's teaching, thus:

> 'Seeing all human beings
> Suffering from pains and distress
> Trying to find deliverance
> And battling against the *māras* (evil demons),
> For the sake of all these living beings
> He proclaims numerous dharmas,
> Using his great skilful means
> He expounds all these sutras.'[45]

---

[42] *Ibid*, p. 126: *tathāgata upāya-kauśalyena trīṇi yānāni deśayati.*

[43] *Ibid*, p. 123. The question follows other declarations that there is one vehicle, and not two or three.

[44] T IX 16b 無量珍寶　不求自得 cf. KSS 117.

[45] T IX 39b 見一切人　受諸苦惱　欲求解脫　與諸魔戰　爲是衆生　說種種法　以大

We then hear that when those who hear are ready for it the 'Dharma-flower', that is, The Lotus Sutra,[46] is also revealed, just as the king finally gave the jewel from his head.

Oddly enough however we find that at the beginning of the parable The Lotus Sutra itself also seems to be described as proclaimed by skilful means. As in many later sections of the sutra there is a stress on the qualities of those who proclaim or keep 'this sutra', meaning The Lotus Sutra, and the verse then continues:

> 'I have attained the Buddha-way,
> And making use of skilful means
> I proclaim this sutra,
> So that they may abide in it.'[47]

The story seems to suggest that The Lotus Sutra is kept back until the end, like the king's jewel; and yet at the same time it is not quite possible to say on the basis of the passages as a whole that the preliminary teachings are skilful means while The Lotus Sutra is not a skilful means. Rather, The Lotus Sutra is given in and through the skilful means and finally becomes apparent, for in the verse quoted the bodhisattvas are already abiding in The Lotus Sutra because of the Buddha's use of skilful means.

The other story, in Chapter VIII, like the story of the son who did not recognise himself, is told not by the Buddha but by his disciples, indeed by no less than five hundred worthy ones ('*arhats*'); though it is not explained whether they spoke in chorus or repeated it one after another. The occasion of the story is that the Buddha has predicted future Buddhahood for all of them, whereupon the story is told to express their feelings of surprise and joy at this. They are compared to a man who went to visit a friend, drank too much and fell asleep. On waking he wanders on to distant parts and finally gets into severe difficulties over feeding and clothing himself. He is content to labour very hard for little reward. Little does he realise that the friend in whose house he had got drunk had sewn a precious jewel into his garment before going off on business. When the friend comes across him again, and points it out to him, his worries are over.

Both the story and the explanation given are relatively brief. The *arhats* had laboured hard for a mere trifle, namely that which they supposed to be

方便　說此諸經 cf. KSS 286. Reference to a sutra within its own text is not unusual as readers are normally urged to keep it, recite it, copy it etc. It may be characteristic of secondary portions of a sutra in terms of its original compilation. There are other reasons for supposing this part to be rather secondary, e.g. reference to 'the city of nirvana' displayed as if it were extinction (T IX 39a 又復賜與涅槃之城言得滅度 cf. KSS 283) which must be a reference to the story in Chapter VII. Since Chapter VII comes before Chapter XIV (or Sanskrit 13) this may not seem surprising, but see also the discussion of compilation questions in Appendix B.

[46] 法華, cf. *passim* 此法華經. *Hokekyō*(法華経)is still the common Japanese name for The Lotus Sutra, though in a formal devotional context *Myōhō Renge Kyō* may be preferred.

[47] T IX 39a 我得佛道　以諸方便　爲說此法　令住其中 cf. KSS 285. *Taishō Shinshū Daizōkyō* has 法 (Dharma), with 經 (Sutra) as a secondary reading. It does not affect the meaning because 'this Dharma' would still imply the previously mentioned 'this Sutra', and therefore 'Sutra' has been kept following KSS to bring out this implication clearly.

nirvana, forgetting in the meanwhile the goal of comprehensive wisdom, or all-knowledge. The Buddha has then declared the provisional nature of their achievement, thus: 'Monks! That which you have obtained is not final extinction. I have long been encouraging you to plant roots of buddha-goodness, and by my skilful means I displayed a form of nirvana. But you supposed it to be the real extinction which you have obtained.'[48] In the verse 'a small part of nirvana' is contrasted with 'real extinction' or 'true extinction'.[49] Thus the main goal of Buddhism is again put into question, or at least people's thinking that they have attained it. The teaching of nirvana is here described explicitly as the Buddha's skilful means. However the most famous story to put across this *critique* is the story of the magic city, which also features a 'place of precious jewels', and to which we now come.

The magic city

The story of the magic city in Chapter VII follows an account of a long-distant previous Buddha's decision to preach. This decision to proclaim the Dharma is presented on the same model as the decision by Gautama Buddha found in Chapter II of the sutra and of course in other Buddhist writings, and the matter will be discussed again below in Chapter Seven. It may be noted now however that the Dharma preached by this ancient Buddha of many aeons ago consisted in the first instance of the four noble truths and the twelve links of dependent origination. As to the teaching of 'The Lotus Flower of the Wonderful Law', this was delivered later at the special request of sixteen bodhisattvas, as the text goes on to relate, who then in their turn are entrusted with its proclamation. The sixteenth of these is identified with the present Buddha in this world. The present Buddha in his turn predicts that there will be further generations who will similarly receive the teaching of nirvana, which will again be followed by the teaching of The Lotus Sutra.

Thus under ever-repeated circumstances there are always these two phases. Firstly there is the initial teaching of Buddhism, the same teaching which the gods entreated the Buddha of antiquity to expound when they said:

> 'World-honoured one, turn the wheel of Dharma,
> Beat the drum of Dharma, sweet as dew,
> Bring across the living beings in suffering and distress,
> Make manifest the way of nirvana.'[50]

---

[48] T IX 29a 諸比丘。汝等所得非究竟滅。我久令汝等種佛善根。以方便故示涅槃相。而汝謂爲實得滅度。cf. KSS 212.

[49] T IX 29b 少涅槃分, contrast 實滅度 and 眞滅. Extinction is meant in the sense of cessation, not annihilation, that is, cessation of karmic force. To some extent the different terminology helps to articulate the argument, but it never stabilised to the extent that 涅槃 (nirvana) came to be seen as a definitely lesser value than 滅度 (extinction). Thus Sakamoto, writing today, can still use one to explain the other thus: 滅とは煩惱の滅した涅槃を指し、即ち究竟眞実の涅槃の意 (*op. cit.* vol. II p. 337, note).

[50] T IX 24c 世尊轉法輪　擊甘露法鼓　度苦惱衆生　開示涅槃道 cf. KSS 183. Note that the same term is used again for nirvana.

This teaching is first given by a Buddha or a Tathāgata because he knows that living beings are strongly attached to pleasures and trifles, because his 'skilful means reaches deeply into the natures of living beings'.[51] It is therefore entirely for their sakes that he proclaims nirvana.[52] As to the second phase, this is the teaching of The Lotus Sutra itself, which assumes the initial teaching of nirvana etc. Under what circumstances does an individual Buddha proclaim The Lotus Sutra? 'If the Tathāgata knows that the time of his nirvana is near, and the assembly is pure, firm in faith and discernment, thoroughly grasping the dharma of voidness and deeply entering into meditation, then he will gather together all the bodhisattvas and *śrāvakas* to proclaim this sutra.'[53] If the present form of The Lotus Sutra is taken as a unity so that Chapter II may be adduced here as indicative of what a Buddha proclaims when it is time to take this step, it may be recalled that the new teaching is not so much a further teaching with separate, extra content. Rather it offers a view of the way in which the initial teaching of nirvana is supposed to be understood. In this further perspective the status of the initial teaching is made problematical, and it is this that the story of the magic city is intended to make clear.

In the story itself a band of travellers is crossing a broad expanse of dangerous country, to a 'Place of Precious Jewels'. They have an experienced guide, but the conditions are so bad and frightening that the travellers get tired out and wish to turn back. The guide finds this regrettable, bearing in mind the treasure which lies ahead of them, and magically creates a city for their rest and encouragement. The travellers enter the city and imagine that they have arrived at their destination (though according to the story it is first presented to them as a temporary resting place). After they have rested, the guide makes the magic city disappear again and summons the travellers onwards to their original goal.

The guide is a man described as having many many skilful means[54] and his creation of the magic city is one such. We may note the conscious deliberation involved: 'The leader, being a man of many many skilful means, reflected thus:'[55] and 'Reflecting thus, by his power of skilful means, he created a magic city more than three hundred *yojanas* across in the middle of their perilous road'.[56]

The interpretation of the story found in the text itself suffers from a slight confusion over twos and threes. The Buddha, who is of course the guide, is said to proclaim two nirvanas by his power of skilful means, so that living beings may stop for rest when they are on the way.[57] If beings get to reside in

[51] T IX 25c 如來方便深入衆生之性 cf. KSS 189f.

[52] T IX 25c 爲是等故說於涅槃 cf. KSS 190.

[53] T IX 25c 若如來自知涅槃時到。衆又清淨信解堅固。了達空法深入禪定。便集諸菩薩及聲聞衆爲說是經。cf. KSS 189.

[54] T IX 26a 導師多諸方便 cf. KSS 190.

[55] T IX 26a 導師多諸方便而作是念 cf. KSS 190.

[56] T IX 26a 作是念已。以方便力。於險道中過三百由旬。化作一城。cf. KSS 190.

[57] T IX 26a 以方便力而於中道爲止息故說二涅槃 cf. KSS 191. This 中道 surely does not mean between the beings of the three worlds and the beings who have transcended the three worlds, as in Sakamoto's note *ad loc.*

either of these 'two places' they are told that the place where they are staying is near to Buddha-insight and that the nirvana which they have attained is not the truly real.[58] We then read the familiar formula 'It is only that the Tathāgata by his power of skilful means, in one Buddha-vehicle differentiates and expounds the three.'[59] This state of affairs is said to be like the guide producing a magic city, which though itself not real is not far from the 'Place of Precious Jewels'. The mention of two nirvanas has led to a flutter of footnotes.[60] Reference to the Sanskrit makes it seem probable that 'two nirvanas' of the *śrāvakas* and of the *pratyekabuddhas* respectively was intended, though this is not explicitly stated in the Chinese.[61] Mention of these two nirvanas and of two places or 'stages'[62] leads on to the standard comment that the Buddha in one vehicle expounds the three. By contrast, the introductory passage, just before the parable is told, does not refer to three, nor, probably, to two in the sense of two preliminaries. When we read: 'There are not two vehicles in the world by which one may attain extinction; there is only the one Buddha-vehicle by which one may attain extinction,'[63] it means that it is incorrect to distinguish between an initial teaching of nirvana and an additional new teaching which would both lead to extinction. The verse explanation of the parable supports this line of thought, as when we read:

> 'The buddhas by their power of skilful means
> Differentiate and expound three vehicles;
> There is only one Buddha-vehicle and
> A second is proclaimed as a resting place.'[64]

Since only one magic city is referred to in the story it might have been simpler if the talk of plural 'nirvanas' and of 'three' had not been introduced to the subsequent explanation. In the discussion of the twos and the threes it is easy to overlook how staggering this proposed way of assessing the teaching of nirvana must have seemed to those who had hitherto taken Buddhist

[58] T IX 26a 所得涅槃非眞實也。cf. KSS 191.

[59] T IX 26c 但是如來方便之力於一佛乘分別說三。cf. KSS 191.

[60] KSS p. 191, footnote, refers back to a previous footnote distinguishing between nirvana with residue and nirvana without residue. However this does not seem to be what is intended here. Sakamoto also gives this possibility, *ad loc.*

[61] Wogihara and Tsuchida, *op. cit.* p. 167 = '*dve nirvāna-bhūmī ... śrāvaka-bhūmim pratyeka-buddha-bhūmim ca.*' KSS and Sakamoto both give this possibility too.

[62] 地, representing Sanskrit *bhūmi*, but in spite of the wider use of this word for the ten stages of bodhisattvahood, it may be infelicitous to translate as 'stage' here because the two 'realms' or 'states' as one might call them, of which it is a question here, are not consecutive ones.

[63] T IX 25c 世間無有二乘而得滅度唯一佛乘得滅度耳。cf. KSS 189. KSS in fact translates '. . . there is no second vehicle . . .', which supports the point being made here, that the passage is not referring to two specific *other* vehicles, that is, to two hinayana vehicles. However the statement also should be taken to mean not that some second vehicle is excluded from the point of view of the buddha-vehicle, but that it is mistaken to differentiate them, from the final point of view of the sutra.

[64] T IX 27b 諸佛方便力　分別說三乘　唯有一佛乘　息處故說二　cf. KSS 198. KSS gives alternative translations, one referring to two vehicles, and one referring to 'a second'.

teaching straightforwardly on the model of, say, the four noble truths. The point of the parable is that the teaching of nirvana as given in the four noble truths etc. is only a restful preliminary to the real attainment required. According to this story it is only by recognising the 'magical' character of that which is at first manifested, that the travellers are able to proceed to real extinction and Buddha-insight. At the same time there is no other picture of 'real extinction' than the original teaching of nirvana. The magic city is *intended* to be mistaken for the place of precious jewels. Nor is the ultimate 'destination' described in any way other than by the same sort of simile as that used for the initial teaching of nirvana, namely as a 'place of precious jewels'. This does not matter. What counts is that the narrative separation of the two draws attention to the provisional character of the initial teaching. This provisional character has to be recognised before its full intent can be realised.

The Buddha's life-span and the story of the physician

The story of the physician is found in Chapter XVI of Kumārajīva's Lotus Sutra, which is Chapter 15 of the Sanskrit manuscript tradition. In historical terms it probably does not represent a primary stage in the sutra's compilation, but once the complete work had come into existence and was translated into Chinese it came to be considered as the most important chapter of all. It is still used liturgically today, along with Chapter II, in a manner representative of the sutra as a whole. The status of the chapter in scholastic discussion and religious practice is not in itself a basis for discussion of it here, but naturally the importance which it acquired is not unconnected with its contents. It certainly does bring to a climax the message of the sutra already examined so far by relating it directly to the person of the Buddha himself. It raises questions about the nature of the Buddha relevant to many discussions of Mahayana Buddhism (which is often misunderstood at this point), and at the same time it contains in the short space of under two pages in the printed *Taishō Shinshū Daizōkyō* no less than ten occurrences of the term *fang-pien* or skilful means. The whole of the subsequent remainder of the sutra only contains another four cases of the term.

Before coming to the story itself some attention must be paid to the opening portion of the text which the story then illustrates, and indeed first of all to the title of the chapter. The title is perhaps best to be translated as 'The Tathāgata's Life-span', although 'Length of Life of the Tathāgata' is also adequate and holds it more literally close to the Sanskrit.[65] It is very

---

[65] T IX 42a 如來壽量 cf. Kern, *op. cit.* p. 298, and Iwamoto, *op. cit.* p. 11 (如来の寿命 の長さ), for *Tathāgatāyuṣ-pramāṇa*. KSS translate 'Revelation of the (Eternal) Life of the Tathāgata', p. 307, clearly preferring to draw upon Dharmarakṣa's 如來現壽品, T IX 113a, and adding the 'Eternal'. A footnote develops this further: 'The revelation of the eternal life of the Buddha in this chapter, which is the most essential of the Buddha's teachings, gave Buddhist belief boundless strength' (p. 307). There is clear reliance here on the idea of the *honbutsu* (本仏), the 'original' or 'fundamental' Buddha, which has a Tendai pedigree, but of

important to notice this precise formulation as well as some others in the body of the text because it is largely on the basis of this chapter that The Lotus Sutra is sometimes represented as replacing the human Buddha with an eternal, transcendent Buddha who is equivalent in his own being to the God of the main theist religions. Such an interpretation is not accurate. The whole purport of this chapter, as will become clear in the details which follow, is to argue that the direct demonstration of the attainment of enlightenment and of nirvana to be seen in the life of the Buddha Śākyamuni (i.e. the historical Buddha) are as much to be understood in terms of the concept of skilful means as his teaching *about* the four noble truths and nirvana. By contrast to the idea that the hero of this tale attained enlightenment after a certain number of years in a historical life, it is said that he had already attained true Buddhahood an incredibly long time previously. The purpose of saying this is to deflate the fixed idea that it took a small number of years. In other words the argument is conceived on an entirely dialectical basis. To think that the text here is gratuitously advancing the conception of an eternal Buddha on the lines of western theism, in a manner which would run contrary to the whole trend of Buddhism in general, both before and after the appearance of this text, would be to misconstrue it entirely.

The term sometimes translated as 'eternal' or 'infinite' means in fact 'immeasurable', and it is crucial to notice the difference.[66] 'Immeasurable' means exactly that one would not in practice be able to measure it; for Maitreya and the others assembled are asked whether supposing vast quantities of worlds were crushed into atoms, and then each atom were carried away from west to east one by one, they would be able to calculate the number of worlds so treated.[67] Of course, they would not be able to, and likewise the length of time which has passed since the Tathāgata attained supreme perfect enlightenment is so long that it cannot be calculated. The same however is true for 'all buddha-tathāgatas', it must be presumed, for this phrase implying the plural reality of many such is used in this very same chapter.[68]

which the exact meaning is possibly obscured by English terms such as 'eternal'. (Cf. also the footnote on the title of chapter XV, KSS 291, where the term 'Eternal Buddha' is explicitly used, presumably for Japanese *honbutsu*.)

[66] T IX 42-3, various cases, but especially 43c 或時爲此衆 說佛壽無量。This clearly brings out the dialectical nature of the proposition: 'At times for all this throng, I proclaim that the Buddha's life is immeasurable'. (cf. KSS 316). 無量 also appears in other Mahayana texts, as a translation of the name Amitāyus, meaning 'Immeasurable life', e.g. in the titles and texts of the 'Pure Land Sutras' 佛說無量壽經 (T360), the 佛說觀無量壽佛經 (T365), and chapter II of T665 which has the same title as Chapter XVI of The Lotus Sutra. The term 無邊, meaning 'boundless', is used only together with 'immeasurable' and should not be construed as having a different implication.

[67] T IX 42b 於意云何。是諸世界。可得思惟校計知其數不。, 'What do you think? Is it possible to imagine and calculate all those worlds so as to know their number or not?' Cf. KSS 308. Compare also the long opening sections of Chapter VII.

[68] T IX 43a 諸佛如來.

The argument of the chapter as a whole arises out of a fantastic event described in the preceding one, Chapter XV.[69] While numerous bodhisattvas are promising that they will protect, read, recite and copy The Lotus Sutra after the passing away of the Buddha, the latter to their great astonishment says that there really is no need for them to be concerned. Why? Because there already are innumerable bodhisattvas ready to do it. These countless bodhisattvas then appear from out of the earth and establish themselves in a marvellous tableau. Not surprisingly this gives rise to considerable per-plexity, and the Buddha assures Maitreya and the original assembly that all of these new arrivals were converted to Buddhism after the Buddha's own enlightenment. Even so, it does not seem possible that so many were con-verted in the mere forty years which have elapsed since the Buddha was enlightened. Maitreya and his disciples say that it is as if a young man of twenty-five were to claim numerous old men as his sons, while the latter recognised him as their father. Since such a thing seems inconceivable they beg the Buddha to explain, and it is this explanation which is given in Chapter XVI on the Tathāgata's life-span.

The preparation for what is about to be said is very similar to that in Chapter II. The disciples are in a state of perplexity, and they must be prepared to receive what will be said with belief and discernment.[70] Three times the Buddha enjoins the disciples to receive his sincerely true word. Three times they promise to listen with belief and discernment. The occasion is solemn.

The Buddha then explains that although he is usually thought of as coming from the Śākya clan and renouncing his palace life, taking up a place of meditation not far from the city of Gayā and there attaining to enlighten-ment, the reality is that innumerable world-systems have come to be and passed away since he originally became a Buddha. Ever since an incon-ceivably long time ago he has been constantly teaching both in this world and in innumerable others. This marvellously different reality is termed 'the Tathāgata's power of mysterious supernatural pervasion' but how, we may ask, is it linked with skilful means.[71] The answer to this is that although the term 'supernatural' or 'divine' is thereafter somewhat neglected, the whole

---

[69] T IX 39c-42a. The account is lengthy and does not need detailed comment as there are no examples of the term skilful means. Apart from being the narrative introduction to chapter XVI it is also the first chapter of the second part of the sutra according to the scholastic division into two equal halves of 14 chapters each. This makes Chapter XVI the main ex-position of the second part, just as chapter II is the main exposition of the first part after a mythical preamble in Chapter I.

[70] T IX 42b 信解, cf. KSS 307. This phrase appeared as the title of Chapter IV.

[71] T IX 42b 如來祕密神通之力 cf. KSS 307-8. The Tendai interpretation of this phrase cited in KSS is anachronistic, however scholastically acceptable, for the *trikāya* doctrine was not yet formulated when The Lotus Sutra was composed. 'Supernatural powers' or 'super-natural pervasion', or perhaps 'divine pervasive power' if theistic connotations are not imported, picks up the Sanskrit term *adiṣṭhāna*, and is sometimes said to be linked with the idea of skilful means. It certainly falls into the general category of qualities and powers acquired by a bodhisattva or a buddha, but as in the case of 'compassion' (*karuṇā*) to which

matter of deflating the historical view of the Buddha's life is explained further in terms of skilful means.

It is as skilful means that various other buddhas such as the Buddha Burning Light (Dīpaṃkara) are differentiated and described as entering nirvana.[72] The various details are framed in accordance with the capacities of those who are to be saved, and 'Again by various skilful means I proclaim the wonderful Dharma which is able to bring joy to the hearts of all the living.'[73] The matter is then related to the historical life-span of the Buddha, for 'Seeing that all living beings take pleasure in lesser teachings[74] and that their virtue is slight while their vileness weighs heavy, to these men I declare that I left home in my youth and attained supreme, perfect enlightenment. But I have really been like this ever since I became a Buddha. I make this proclamation only as skilful means to teach living beings and get them to enter the Buddha-way.'[75] In this way the understanding of Buddhist teaching in terms of skilful means which has already been more or less systematically advanced throughout the sutra is here applied to the Buddha's own life-story.

It is not surprising that this is applied to the end of the Buddha's life as well as to its opening, and so we read, 'Although it is at this time not a real extinction, nevertheless I announce my impending extinction. It is by this skilful means that the Tathāgata teaches and transforms the living.'[76] If the teaching of the Buddha's enlightenment is conceived and put forward to display the possibility of not being mentally entangled in trifles, the demonstration of his extinction, contrived though it is, is similarly necessary to prevent people from becoming complacent as a result of the Buddha's presence. In other words this too is dialectically conceived to take account of

the same general considerations apply, direct correlations with *upāyakauśalya* are not common. At any rate in the texts studied here, *fang-pien* and *fang-pien-li* either enjoy a prominence of their own or are linked most frequently with the 'insight' of buddhas or of bodhisattvas. As seen below, this present discussion of the Buddha's life-span, while drawing in 神通 in an incidental way, proceeds in terms of *fang-pien*.

Chapter XXVII of The Lotus Sutra stresses supernatural powers rather than skilful means (which there appears once only, and that in a list of seven *pāramitās* and other qualities, T IX 59c). By supernatural powers two princes show their contempt for spatial limitations and thereby convert their father the king to Buddhism. This emphasis on magical tricks is an important part of Mahayana Buddhism, and is no doubt in many ways parallel to the exercise of skilful means. However, although it also undermines any dependence on pedestrian literalism in understanding Buddhism, it does not lead into the profound central critique of religious language brought about by the sustained discussion of skilful means in The Lotus Sutra as a whole.

[72] T IX 42b-c 我說燃燈佛等。又復言其入於涅槃。如是皆以方便分別。cf. KSS 309.

[73] T IX 42c 又以種種方便說微妙法。能令衆生發歡喜心。cf. KSS 309.

[74] Lesser teachings, (dharmas) 小法; or small things, trifles.

[75] T IX 42c 見諸衆生樂於小法德薄垢重者。爲是人說。我少出家得阿耨多羅三藐三菩提。然我實成佛已來久遠若斯。但以方便教化衆生。令入佛道作如是說。cf. KSS 309f.

[76] T IX 42c 然今非實滅度。而便唱言當取滅度。如來以方便教化衆生。cf. KSS 311. In this case the term 滅 is used for extinction as skilful means, as well as for 'real' extinction. Often the term 涅槃 is used for the straightforwardly announced nirvana, as for the Buddha Dīpaṃkara (note 72 above). This present case means that no quite constant usage developed.

the psychological trends of living beings. Thus the Tathāgata is said to teach by skilful means that the appearance of buddhas in the world is very rare.[77] This is a widespread idea in Buddhist writings but it takes on a particular strength here because it is conceived in terms of skilful means.[78] Skilful means is the technical term which defines any particular piece of Buddhist teaching as being contrived in accordance with the dispositions of those who are to hear it. And, to return to the Buddha's nirvana, 'That is why the Tathāgata, though he does not really become extinct, announces his extinction.'[79]

In this way therefore, both the two key points in the life of the Buddha, his enlightenment and his nirvana, are given out as skilful means in accordance with the needs of the living, for their deliverance. This is certainly the main thrust of the exposition when it is stated straightforwardly. It is this same point which is conveyed in the teaching that the length of the Tathāgata's life is of unimaginable and indefinite length. Let it be observed once again that it is not a question of there being no beginning at all to the Buddha's career as a Buddha, and neither is there any suggestion that the ultimate resolution is anything other than a genuine nirvana or extinction. It is in the context of the Buddha's teaching in many diverse ways that we read: 'Thus it is that since I became a Buddha in the very far distant past, my lifetime continues to persist without extinction through immeasurable *asaṃkhyeya kalpas*. Good sons! The lifetime which I attained originally by practising the bodhisattva-way is even now not yet finished and will still be twice what it was so far.'[80] This dramatisation of the immense length of a bodhisattva's, and a buddha's career is in effect being used as a narrative argument about the nature of the concepts of enlightenment and of nirvana.

The fundamental conception of the Buddha's teaching activity here moves between the same two poles which characterised it in the earlier chapters. On the one hand the dispositions of the living are varied and not altogether praiseworthy, and hence the Buddha 'teaches in a variety of ways, with karmic reasonings, parables and diverse terminology.'[81] At the same time 'The Tathāgata knows and sees the character of the triple world as it really is: no birth-and-death, no going away, no coming forth, no being in the world and no extinction, no reality and no falsehood, no being thus and no being

---

[77] T IX 42c-43a 是故如來以方便說。比丘當知。諸佛出世難可值遇。cf. KSS 311.

[78] Cf. also Chapter XXVII where a buddha is said to be as rare as the *udumbara* flower, and should therefore be visited when the occasion presents itself (see KSS p. 426), and also Chapter II where the preaching of The Lotus Sutra Dharma is said to be as rare as the *udumbara* flower (see KSS p. 43). The point is always related to human expectations. Buddhas could appear more often, it is implied, but familiarity would lead to indifference, and hence a contrived specialness, contrived by skilful means, has to be maintained. Cf. also Chapter II, KSS 66.

[79] T IX 43a 是故如來。雖不實滅而言滅度。cf. KSS 311.

[80] T IX 42c 如是我成佛已來甚大久遠。壽命無量阿僧祇劫常住不滅。諸善男子。我本行菩薩道所成壽命。今猶未盡復倍上數。cf. KSS 310-11.

[81] T IX 42c 以若干因緣譬喩言辭種種說法。cf. KSS 310. This phrase occurs many times, especially in Chapter II, and indicates that the basic idea is really the same throughout the sutra, namely that Buddhism is a collection of different forms of teaching devised to communicate it to those who do not yet understand the point of it directly for themselves. 'Karmic reasonings', a free rendering for 因緣: explanations of causality in human experience.

otherwise. Unlike the view of the triple world held within the triple world itself, the Tathāgata clearly sees such things as these without mistake.'[82] To claim that something like monotheism is here asserted would be to maintain a view worse than those which the triple world normally maintains about itself. On the contrary, the last-quoted sentence keeps The Lotus Sutra firmly in the same area as the Perfection of Insight literature. It is this understanding of the nature of the world which subverts the standard view of the activity of a buddha. The standard view is provisionally accepted and encouraged through skilful means, but there comes a time when it is also necessary to indicate the redundancy of the terms in which the teaching is couched.

The initial exposition of Chapter XVI considered above is followed by a story to illustrate the argument. A physician is travelling abroad and in the meantime his sons drink some poisonous medicines and become delirious. When he returns he prepares good medicine for them. The ones who take the good medicine recover, but the others have quite lost their senses and refuse to take the good medicine. The father reflects, and decides upon a skilful means[83] to make them take it. He warns them that he is very old and approaching death, then leaves for another country from where he sends a messenger back to report that he has died. The sons are overcome with grief, come to their senses and take the medicine which he had prepared. Hearing this the father returns and they are reunited. Immediately following the story the question is raised as to whether the physician in this case was guilty of a falsehood, and the answer returned is that he was not. Then the Buddha declares: 'I also am like this. Since I became a Buddha, infinite, boundless, hundred thousand millions of *nayutas* of *asaṃkhyeya kalpas* ago, for the sake of all the living I have declared by my power of skilful means that I must enter nirvana, and yet no one can rightly say that I have perpetrated a falsehood.'[84]

Since the story is not further explained in the prose text it must be taken as directly illustrating the argument already pursued before. The invented death of the physician puts the nirvana of the Buddha firmly at the level of provisional truth designed to match the psychological needs of the Buddha's followers. This is supported, it may be observed, by the story context of medicine and healing, a common way of conceiving the nature of Buddhism.

---

[82] T IX 42c 如來如實知見三界之相。無有生死若退若出。亦無在世及滅度者。非實非虛非如非異。不如三界見於三界。如斯之事。如來明見無有錯謬。cf. KSS 310. 'No reality and no falsehood' may seem strange in view of the many protestations that what the Buddha says is 'real' or 'true' (實) and not 'false' (虛) However, the point is that it is only necessary to say that the Buddha's teaching is true and not false when someone is perplexed about the possibility of an inconsistency or falsehood in it.   At such a time the initial differentiation between 'real' and 'false' is on the side of the person so perplexed, and is not part of the Buddha's own view of the triple world.

[83] T IX 43a 我今當設方便 cf. KSS 313. Note the conscious reflection involved here.

[84] T IX 43b 我亦如是。成佛已來。無量無邊百千萬億那由他阿僧祇劫。爲衆生故。以方便力言當滅度。亦無有能如法說我虛妄過者。cf. KSS 313-4.

The physician is 'wise and perspicacious, conversant with medical art and
skilled in healing all sorts of diseases.'[85] The fundamental condition of the
sons is one of health, and it is only the foolish imbibing of poison which makes
the antidote necessary. The physician prepares the antidote, which is not
otherwise necessary in itself. This is entirely consistent with the diagnosis-
prescription pattern of the four noble truths, and indicates the pragmatic
rather than speculative intention of Buddhism which has often been noted.
This chapter, and this story, really represent a radicalisation of such an
understanding of the Buddhist religion, because the Buddha's own entry into
nirvana (that is, his death at the end of a life-span of eighty years) is now
treated as being a supreme skilful means to bring about regret and self-
examination on the part of the living. The Buddha's influence is thenceforth
not to be directly viewed, but is said to be continued only indirectly, in order
to maintain the impressive story of his birth, his enlightenment and his death.

The concluding verses twice confirm that the Buddha's nirvana is given
out as a skilful means to bring about right attitudes among the living. One of
these cases explicitly brings in relic-worship under this umbrella, thus:

> 'By skilful means I manifest nirvana
> Though really I am not extinct . . .
> They all look on me as extinct
> And everywhere worship my relics,
> All cherishing tender emotions
> As their hearts begin to thirst with hope.'[86]

This is important as bringing in the main focal point of Buddhist devotions
from earliest times to the context of the thought of skilful means. It is not
only doctrinal concepts which are to be understood as skilful means but also
ritual practice.

When the time is ripe and the people are ready in themselves the Buddha
is said to reveal himself again, and here at last quite ambiguously:

> 'And then I tell all living beings
> That I am always present here without extinction;
> I use my power of skilful means
> To manifest both extinction and non-extinction.'[87]

The observer cannot idly observe that the Buddha is extinct or not.

The pragmatic, soteriological criterion for every form of Buddhist teaching
finds clear expression in the closing verses of the chapter:

> 'I always know all living beings,
> Whether they practice the way or do not practice it;
> In accordance with what is required for their salvation

---

[85] T IX 43a 智慧聰達明練方藥善治衆病。cf. KSS 312. 'Wise' here for 智慧 (= insight),
following KSS.

[86] 方便現涅槃　而實不滅度...衆見我滅度　廣供養舍利　咸皆懷戀慕　而生渇仰心
cf. KSS 314. A distinction between 涅槃 and 滅度 is first apparent here, but then obscured.

[87] T IX 43b 我時語衆生　常在此不滅　以方便力故　現有滅不滅 cf. KSS 315.

I proclaim for their sakes a variety of teachings;
I am always considering in my own mind
What I can do to bring the living beings
To enter the unsurpassed way
And speedily accomplish their Buddhahood.'[88]

From all that has been said above, we may conclude that the Mahayana articulation of Buddhism as a working religion along these lines is altogether controlled by the concept of skilful means.

---

[88] T IX 44a 我常知衆生　行道不行道　隨所應可度　爲說種種法　每自作是意　以何 令衆生　得入無上慧　速成就佛身 cf. KSS 317.

4 MYTHOLOGY AND SKILFUL MEANS IN THE LOTUS SUTRA

Illumination of all worlds

So far the more fantastic perspectives of The Lotus Sutra have been rather left on one side in favour of the more direct expository account in Chapter II and the string of illustrative stories which follow. This procedure is justified in that the account given so far has followed the main lines of exposition apparent in the sutra itself while paying special attention to the usage of the term skilful means. Readers of the sutra however will be aware that the overall scenario of this exposition includes quantities of mythological elaboration in which indeed western readers with none too much time sometimes get lost. Perhaps it is best to admit that the overall narrative framework by no means affords the dramatic coherence sometimes claimed for it, which is not surprising in view of the fact that it was undoubtedly the work of various hands over a long period of time.

Nevertheless the mythological perspective in which this sutra is cast, as indeed is Mahayana Buddhism in general, cannot be overlooked, and it has already appeared above in various incidental ways. People sometimes have the impression that Mahayana Buddhism is mainly an elaboration of the more fantastic elements of popular Buddhism, but this is a serious misunderstanding. In fact such elaboration is quite possible without any accompanying presence of the main thrust of the Mahayana, as can be seen in a generally contemporaneous work, The Mahāvastu, which shows much mythological enthusiasm but little intellectual penetration.[1] Mythological elements in Mahayana Buddhism are always related in the last analysis to its central

[1] Jones, J. J. trans. *The Mahāvastu* 3 vols. Pali Text Society, London 1949, 1952 and 1956 respectively, and Basak, Dr. R. ed. *Mahāvastu Avadāna*, 3 vols, Calcutta 1963ff. This work was compiled over a long period. Some parts have important parallels with the Pali Canon, explored by Windisch in *Die Komposition des Mahāvastu* (Abhandlungen der philologisch-historischen Klasse d. K. sächsischen Gesellschaft der Wissenschaften Bd. XXIV No. XIV, 1909), while other parts, such as the extended discussion of ten *bhūmis* or stages in the career of a bodhisattva, may be later than the initial conception of Mahayana Buddhism. The Mahāvastu makes an interesting comparison with The Lotus Sutra, etc. because it is fully developed mythologically but without any central emphasis on insight and skilful means, and hence without any critique whatever of the received Buddhist tradition. Thus the famous account of the *lokottara* character of the Buddha remains mere supernaturalism, unlike the understanding of the Buddha in The Lotus Sutra, and unlike the disguises of Vimalakīrti (see more below). On the other hand the mythological elaboration, especially the projection of large numbers of buddhas, tends to subvert a pedestrian view of Buddhist doctrine, and hence to call for the conceptual break-through offered by the Mahayana. In this sense it is indeed a bridge work, as has often been remarked, though of course not in a tidy chronological sense. Various other references to this work will be found below.

grasp of what Buddhism means and how it works. One might argue long about what is orthodox and what is not, but a fair historical perspective has to recognise that this central grasp represents a plausible and respectworthy *possible* continuation of early Buddhism. It is neither a rationalisation which refuses to entertain mythological concepts nor a submersion in waves of irrelevant fantasy. This is not the place for a general account of mythology in Buddhism, but it so happens that three chapters of some importance in the Lotus Sutra, chapters I, XI and XXV, make use of the term skilful means in a manner which throws light on this subject. It must be admitted that in each of these chapters the term occurs once only, but each case is in fact a significant one, by contrast with its very occasional and incidental use in some other chapters. As the third of these chapters is about the famous bodhisattva Avalokitésvara, it will be convenient to follow up with some attention to another less known bodhisattva, Pūrṇa, who appears in Chapter VIII of The Lotus Sutra amidst the only cluster of references to skilful means still not otherwise discussed. It will be convenient to mention also *en passant* one or two aspects of The Mahāvastu and of a Mahayana writing, The Śūraṃgama-samādhi Sutra, which was translated by Kumārajīva. This approach provides a general context for the very special bodhisattva Vimalakīrti, who is the main figure in the text to be explained in Chapter Five below.

Those impatient with the prolific imagery of Mahayana sutras might dismiss the opening chapter of The Lotus Sutra as a wearisome preamble of little doctrinal interest. The Buddha himself does not begin to speak until Chapter II. Nevertheless what the Buddha is said to have done is as important for the understanding of Buddhism as what he is purported to have taught in words and although in this case the action is mythic in quality, the meaning of the myth is partially explicated within the narrative itself by the bodhisattva Mañjuśrī. Mañjuśrī is especially noted for his insight, and his recollection of past Buddha-events enables him to interpret those of the present. His explanation provides the link between the opening phantasmagoria of Chapter I and the doctrinal expositions of Chapter II.

The sutra first describes the Buddha enthroned in state amid a vast multitude of devotees including gods, dragons, humans and many others. First he preached 'the sutra of innumerable meanings'[2] and entered 'the *samādhi* of innumerable meanings'[3] (on which more below). He then sent forth from the circle of white hair between his eyebrows the ray of light which spurred on the throng to question his intention. The bodhisattva Maitreya asked the bodhisattva Mañjuśrī if he was able to explain it. The latter said it

---

[2] T IX 2b 無量義經, cf. KSS 6. In full: 爲諸菩薩說大乘經。名無量義敎菩薩法佛所護念。 'For the sake of all the bodhisattvas he preached the Mahayana sutra called "the innumerable meanings", the Dharma for teaching bodhisattvas preserved and kept in mind by the buddhas.'
[3] T IX 2b 入於無量義處三昧 cf. KSS 6.

indicated that the Buddha intended to proclaim 'the great Dharma'[4] and
explained his interpretation by narrating the previous parallel occasion under
the Buddha known as Sun-Moon-Light-Tathāgata.[5] This flashback technique,
technically known as an *avadāna*, provides the narrative framework for the
chapter as a whole. Maitreya and Mañjuśrī themselves figure within the story
under different names and the present Buddha is clearly a new exemplar of
the previous one. Only one case is referred to in detail, but the reader is given
to understand that there was not merely one such former occasion but rather
an impressively recessive series. The Buddhas named Sun-Moon-Light num-
bered no less than 20,000.[6] Indeed Mañjuśrī himself pronounces the principle
in numberless generality: 'Whenever from any of the former Buddhas I have
seen this auspice, after emitting such a ray, they have thereupon preached the
great Dharma.'[7]

The term 'skilful means' itself occurs but once only in the whole of Chapter
I, and that right at the end of the stanzas. It does not occur in the equivalent
prose passage. Yet in spite of its infrequency the term is here closely and
importantly linked with the central symbol of the whole piece, namely the
ray of light which marvellously issues from the circle of white hair between
the eyebrows of the Buddha. On account of this link the whole mythological
preamble emerges as an indirect anticipation of the teaching of the sutra as a
whole.

Since Mañjuśrī can remember the significance of the light sent out in all
directions by the ancient 'Buddha of Light', he is able to understand the
intention of the present Buddha when he does likewise. 'The present sign is
like the previous omen',[8] or, in the prose equivalent, it is 'no different'.[9] What
does the sign mean? In brief it means that the Buddha desires to preach the
'Law Flower Sutra', that is, The Lotus Sutra.[10] Or again 'The present Buddha
sends forth a ray of light, to help to reveal the meaning of true reality'.[11]

[4] T IX 3c 大法 cf. KSS 19. Also described in this context as 雨大法雨。吹大法螺。擊大
法鼓。演大法義。'pouring down the rain of the great dharma, blowing the conch of the great
dharma, beating the drum of the great dharma, and expounding the meaning of the great
dharma'. The 'meaning' here certainly picks up the phrase 'innumerable meanings': the
innumerable meanings turn out to have 'a' meaning.

[5] T IX 3c 日月燈明如來, cf. KSS 19, i.e. Candrasūryapradīpatathāgata.

[6] T IX 3c 如是二萬佛。皆同一字。號日月燈明。cf. KSS 21, etc.

[7] T IX 3c 我於過去諸佛曾見此瑞。放斯光已即說大法。cf. KSS 19.

[8] T IX 5b 今相如本瑞 cf. KSS 31.

[9] T IX 4b 今見此瑞與本無異。cf. KSS 25, 'Now I see that this auspice is no different
from the former one.'

[10] T IX 5b 法華經 cf. KSS 31, and in the prose, T IX 4b 妙法蓮華經 'The Sutra of the Lotus
of the Wonderful Dharma,' cf. KSS 25. This latter of course is the same as the name of the
sutra as translated by Kumārajīva, Ch. *Miao-Fa Lien-hua Ching* or J. *Myōhō Renge Kyō*.
The narrative context links this with the 'Great Dharma' referred to earlier (see note 4 above);
this implies that it is The Lotus Sutra which gives 'the meaning' of the previous teaching in
many meanings.

[11] T IX 5b 今佛放光明　助發實相義 cf. KSS 31. 'Now the Buddha . . .' is in fact parallel
to the previous verse 'the present sign . . .'(今相), and therefore I prefer to translate 'The
present Buddha' which maintains the parallelism with previous buddhas. Cf. Sakamoto, *op.
cit.* Vol. I p. 64: 今の相 and 今の仏.

There is a suggestive indirectness about the phrase, 'to help to reveal the meaning of true reality', and this may be compared with the rather non-committal explanation partially quoted already and which in full runs: 'The present sign is like the former auspice; it is a skilful means of the buddhas'.[12] The sign is itself an effective symbol of revelation, but it is not to be idly identified with that to which it tends. The ray of light illumines the whole conditioned world, and yet 'the Lotus of the Wonderful Dharma' has not thereby been proclaimed, or at least not yet. Since this ray of light, this sign, which dominates the whole opening scene of the sutra, is explicitly identified as a skilful means, we may take it that the subordinate details are also to be understood in this light.

Two perspectives emerge. Firstly this miraculous ray of light, a skilful means of the buddhas, illuminates conditioned existence in all its multiplicity and correlates it with the consistent intention of the buddhas. Secondly, the present Buddha is linked through this skilful means with previous buddhas in a series of recurrent patterns. There is a mutual interaction and support between these buddhas stringing through the whole universe which takes especially interesting form in Chapter XI (see again below).

The one ray of light illuminates countless worlds, or so one may fairly gloss, for eighteen thousand is as good as countless when it comes to counting worlds. The ray itself is but 'a single ray',[13] 'a single pure ray',[14] and 'a great ray universally radiated'.[15] Yet this one ray of light 'illuminated eighteen thousand worlds in the eastern quarter, so that there was nowhere it did not reach'.[16] It touched the lowest hells and the highest heavens, displaying the karmic condition of living beings in all the six states, and illuminating the work of countless buddhas and bodhisattvas. Even the sutras or teachings of all those buddhas could be clearly heard.[17] The picture is developed in some detail in both prose and verse, but may be summed up in the verse:

> 'Rare are the supernatural powers
> And insight of the buddhas;
> Sending forth a single ray
> They illuminate innumerable domains.'[18]

[12] T IX 5b 今相如本瑞　是諸佛方便 cf. KSS 31.

[13] T IX 3b 一光 cf. KSS 17.

[14] T IX 3c 一淨光 cf. KSS 18.

[15] T IX 2b 大光普照 cf. KSS 9.

[16] T IX 2b 照東方萬八千世界。靡不周遍。cf. KSS 7.

[17] T IX 2b, cf. KSS 7, 'sutras or teachings or sutra dharmas': 經法 sutra teachings or sutra dharmas, apparently just 'dharmas' in the Sanskrit (cf. Wogihara and Tsuchida *op. cit.* p. 4).

[18] T IX 3c 諸佛神力　智慧希有　放一淨光　照無量國 cf. KSS 17f. 'Domains' here for 國 which more literally would be 'countries', but cf. the previous expression 國界, and indeed earlier 世界 (cf. note 16 above). Dharmarakṣa has 佛土 at this point, T IX 63c. All these refer to a 'world' in which a Buddha is active, a *buddha-kṣetra*, cf. Étienne Lamotte's extended discussion in *L'Enseignement de Vimalakīrti*, Louvain 1962, pp. 395 ff. Note also the correlation of supernatural powers 神力 with insight 智慧, so that the former takes a position analogous to that of skilful means; and cf. earlier discussion of 神通 in Chapter Three, note 71.

This illuminating ray however is not mere idle magic, nor a display of super-natural power for its own sake. It is related to the many ways in which existence is provisionally understood.

It was mentioned earlier that the emission of the ray of light is preceded in Kumārajīva's version by reference to a 'sutra of innumerable meanings' and a *'samādhi* of innumerable meanings'.[19] The pedigree of these phrases is obscure as it finds no precise confirmation in Dharmarakṣa's version nor in the available Sanskrit.[20] The traditional association with a specific text known as the *Wu liang i ching* (J. *Muryōgikyō*) is also of little help as this latter text was probably produced in China some time after Kumārajīva's text was completed, possibly indeed because someone thought 'it' *ought* to be extant.[21] The 'sutra of innumerable meanings' is also described as a *mahāyāna* sutra, this again being peculiar to Kumārajīva's translation.[22] The implication is that there is a great vehicle sutra or teaching which purveys an endless variety of meanings. The great exposition is consistent yet variegated. Similarly, in the case of the *samādhi*, the Buddha is said to sit cross-legged, 'his body and mind motionless',[23] yet cognisant of the innumerable meanings. The narrative repetition about the fomer Buddha has a parallel statement.[24] The verse passage adds that the 'sutra of innumerable meanings' was preached among the 'hosts of living beings',[25] and that it is for their sakes 'broadly differentiated'.[26] In spite of this extensive differentiation it is a single sutra and is linked with a single *samādhi*. Their stress on consistency in variety foreshadows a central theme of the whole sutra. It is thoroughly reinforced by the imagery of the single ray of light radiating through all aspects of existence. Indeed it is out of the concentrated mental state des-cribed as the *samādhi* of innumerable meanings that the marvellous ray of light is sent forth.

[19] References in notes 2 and 3 above.

[20] Cf. T IX 63b.

[21] This is T276. See also next note.

[22] Dharmarakṣa refers to 'the extended verses' 方等大頌, T IX 63b, cf. Wogihara and Tsuchida *op. cit.* p. 4 '. . . *mahānirdeśaṃ nāma dharma-paryāyaṃ sūtrāntaṃ mahā-vaipulyaṃ . .*' These differences do not really affect the main argument below, though they do show that the basis for accepting the *Wu Liang I Ching* as being what is referred to here is very shaky indeed. Originally it must have referred in a general way to previous teaching by the Buddha, then particularly to extended teaching vouchsafed to bodhisattvas. The English translation now available (see Chapter Two, note 63) adopts the position that this sutra is an introduction to The Lotus Sutra, according to the T'ien T'ai (J. Tendai) tradition assumed in the KSS footnote on page 6. There is no Sanskrit original for this text, and it seems most unlikely that the Sanskrit referred to a specific writing as the 'Mahānirdeśa'. The alternative title 'Ami-tartha' is simply a retrospective construct based on the Chinese, belonging to that class of invented titles for which Nanjio's catalogue of the Chinese Tripitaka is rightly criticised by the editors of *Hōbōgirin*.

[23] T IX 2b 身心不動 cf. KSS 6.

[24] T IX 4a, cf. KSS 22.

[25] T IX 4b 於諸大衆中 cf. KSS 25. The implication of this is that what is preached would be Mahayana in a broad sense and not in the narrower technical sense of that which is preached among bodhisattvas only.

[26] T IX 4b 而爲廣分別 cf. KSS 25.